USDA

United States
Department of
Agriculture

Forest Service

Northern
Research Station

Resource Bulletin
NRS-69

# Nebraska Timber Industry: An Assessment of Timber Product Output and Use

# 2009

Brian F. Walters
Dennis M. Adams
Ronald J. Piva

## Abstract

In 2009 there were 62 active primary wood-processing mills in Nebraska. These mills processed 4.1 million cubic feet of industrial roundwood. There was 4.09 million cubic feet of industrial roundwood harvested from Nebraska forests. The majority of roundwood harvested was for saw logs, accounting for 72 percent of the total. The harvesting of industrial roundwood products generated 1.5 million cubic feet of harvest residues. Primary wood-processing mills generated 68,000 green tons of mill residues.

## Cover Photo

Mill yard log deck. Photo by U.S. Forest Service, bugwood.org.

# Contents

# INTRODUCTION

Nebraska's wood products manufacturing industry[1] employs more than 2,300 workers and has an output of more than $362 million (U.S. Census Bureau 2007). Given the importance of this industry to the economy of Nebraska, this bulletin analyzes recent forest industry trends and reports the results of a detailed study of forest industry, industrial roundwood production, and associated primary mill wood and bark residue in 2009. Such detailed information is necessary for intelligent planning and decisionmaking in wood procurement, economic research, forest resources management, and forest industry development.

The last published report of timber product output and use in Nebraska (Piva and Adams 2008) covered a 2006 study and is used here for comparison. When new surveys are completed, errors and omissions from previous surveys are corrected. As a result of our ongoing efforts to improve the survey's efficiency and reliability, changes may have been made to the previous survey's data. All comparisons and analysis in this report are based on the reprocessed data from earlier surveys, which may not match earlier published data. Rows and columns of supporting tables may not sum due to rounding, but data in each table cell are accurately displayed.

Information about the forest resources of Nebraska is available at the FIA Web site: http://nrs.fs.fed.us/fia/data-tools/state-reports/NE.

*The Authors*

*BRIAN F. WALTERS is a forester with the Forest Inventory and Analysis (FIA) program at the Northern Research Station in St. Paul, MN. He received a B.S. in forestry in 2005 and an M.S. in geographic information science in 2008 from Michigan State University.*

*DENNIS M. ADAMS is the Rural Forestry Program Leader, Nebraska Forest Service (NFS), University of Nebraska-Lincoln (UNL). He received a B.S. in forest management from Iowa State University in 1968 and an M.S. in horticulture and forestry from UNL in 1977. He has served as a forester with the NFS, UNL since 1973.*

*RONALD J. PIVA is a forester with the FIA program at the Northern Research Station in St. Paul, MN. He received a B.S. in forest management from the University of Missouri-Columbia in 1984 and joined the Forest Service in 1987.*

---

[1]North American Industry Classification System (NAICS) 321–wood product manufacturing.

## STUDY METHODS

This study was a cooperative effort between the Nebraska Forest Service (NFS) and the Forest Inventory and Analysis (FIA) unit at the Northern Research Station (NRS) of the U.S. Forest Service. The FIA program is responsible for providing forest resource statistics, including timber product outputs, for all ownerships across the United States.

NFS personnel surveyed all known primary wood-using mills, using questionnaires supplied by NRS. The questionnaires were designed to determine the size and composition of the State's primary wood-using industry, its use of roundwood, and its generation and disposition of wood residues. Completed questionnaires were sent to NRS for processing and analyses. As part of data processing, all industrial roundwood volumes reported on the questionnaires were converted to standard units of measure using regional conversion factors (Table 1). Timber removals by source of material and harvest residues generated during logging were estimated from standard product volumes using factors developed from logging utilization studies previously conducted by NRS. To provide a complete assessment of Nebraska's timber product output, data on roundwood volume processed by mills in Nebraska (receipts) were loaded into a regional timber removals database where they were supplemented with data on roundwood exported outside the State.

Certain terms used in this report -- retained, exports, imports, production, and receipts -- have specialized meanings and relationships unique to the FIA program that surveys timber product output (TPO) (Fig. 1; Appendix).

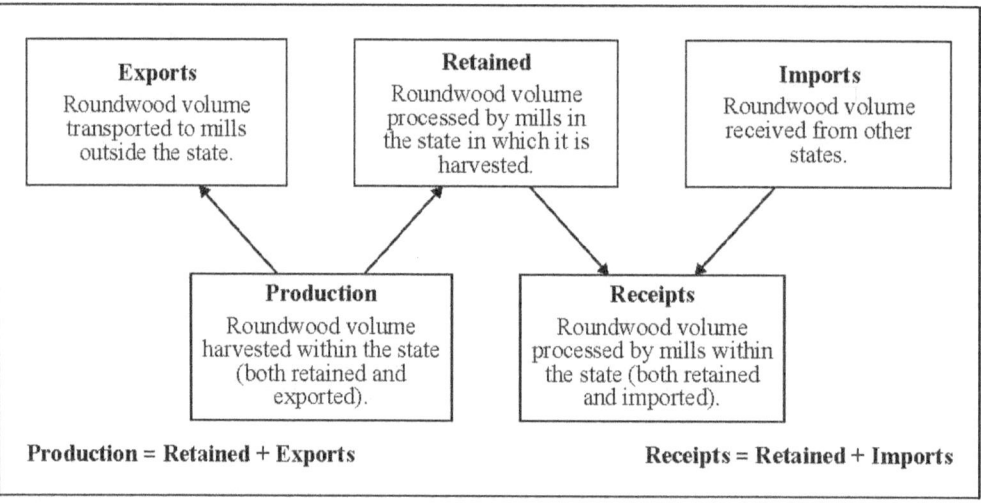

Figure 1.—The movement of industrial roundwood.

Table 1.—Conversion factors from reported unit of measure to standard unit of measure[a]

| | Reported unit of measure | | | | | |
|---|---|---|---|---|---|---|
| Product (Standard unit of measure) | International ¼-inch rule MBF | Doyle scale MBF | Green tons | Standard cords | Thousand pieces | Thousand cubic feet |
| **Saw logs and handles** (MBF International ¼-inch rule) | 1 | 1.38 | 0.2174 | 0.5 | -- | 0.158 |
| **Veneer logs and cooperage** (MBF International ¼-inch rule) | 1 | 1.14 | 0.2174 | 0.5 | -- | 0.158 |
| **Pulp and composite products, and industrial fuelwood** (Standard cords) | -- | -- | 0.4167 | 1 | -- | 0.079 |
| **Poles** (Pieces) | 20 | -- | 4.348 | 10 | 1,000 | 1 |
| **Posts** (Thousand pieces) | 0.2 | -- | 0.04167 | 0.1 | 1 | 0.0079 |
| **Cabin logs, excelsior/shavings, and miscellaneous products** (Thousand cubic feet) | 0.158 | 0.21804 | 0.0329193 | 0.079 | 7.9 | 0.79 |
| **Cabin logs, excelsior/shavings, and miscellaneous products** (Thousand cubic feet) | 0.158 | 0.21804 | 0.17604 | 0.0329193 | 7.9 | 1 |

[a] Reported volume times conversion factor = standard volume. For example, a sawmill reports receiving 100 MBF Doyle rule of roundwood; to convert that to MBF International ¼-inch rule: 100 * 1.38 = 138 MBF.

# PRIMARY TIMBER INDUSTRY IN NEBRASKA
## Industrial Roundwood

- Nebraska's primary wood-using industry included 57 sawmills, 1 veneer mill, 3 post, pole, and piling mills, and 1 mill that produced other products (Table 2, Fig. 2).

- Receipts of industrial roundwood at Nebraska primary wood-using mills totaled 4.1 million cubic feet in 2009, a decrease of 19 percent from the 5.1 million cubic feet received in 2006 (Table 3).

- Ninety percent of the industrial roundwood processed by Nebraska's primary wood-using mills was harvested from forests within the State. Iowa was the largest supplier of out-of-State wood, supplying nearly 10 percent of the total industrial roundwood processed (Table 4).

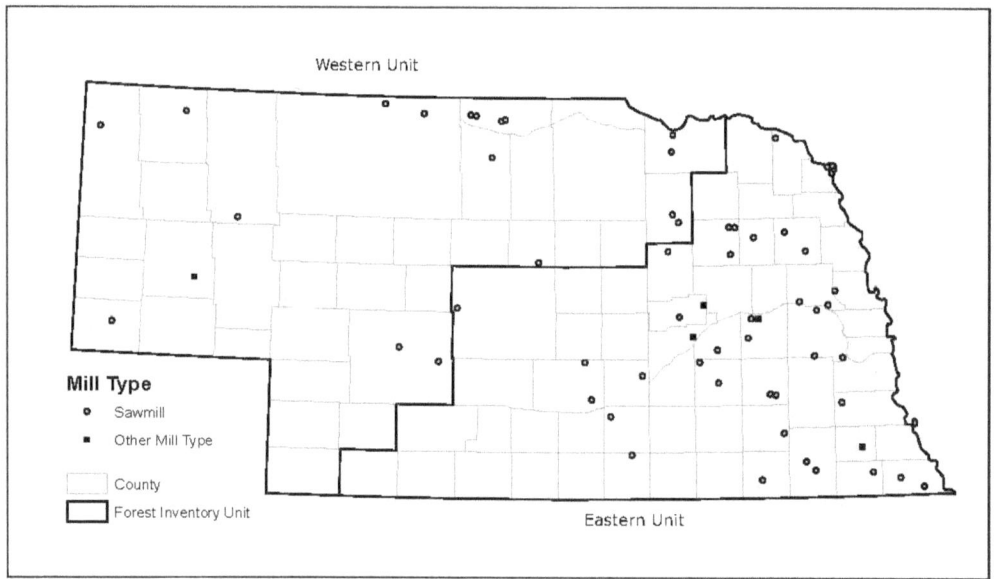

Figure 2.—Nebraska Forest Inventory Units and approximate locations of primary wood-using mills, 2009.

- Eighty-nine percent of the industrial roundwood processed by Nebraska primary wood-using mills was composed of hardwood species. Cottonwood alone accounted for 83 percent of the total volume processed. Softwoods accounted for 11 percent of the volume processed, and most of that was cedar/juniper.

- Industrial roundwood production decreased by 33 percent between 2006 and 2009, from 6.1 million cubic feet to 4.1 million cubic feet (Table 5, Fig. 3).

- Ninety-one percent of industrial roundwood harvested in Nebraska was retained for processing by primary wood-using mills in the State. Mills in Wyoming, Iowa, South Dakota, Missouri, and other countries received Nebraska's industrial roundwood exports (Table 6).

4

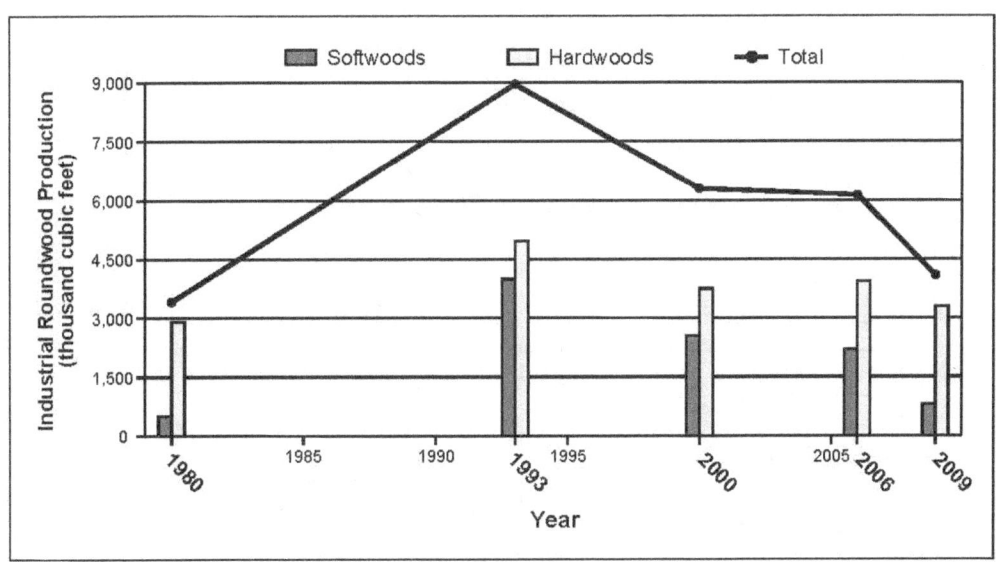

Figure 3.—Industrial roundwood production by major species group and survey year, Nebraska (Blyth et al. 1984, Hackett and Adams 1996, Reading and Adams 2002, Piva and Adams 2008).

- Seventy-five percent of the industrial roundwood production volume was from the cottonwood species group. Ponderosa pine (10 percent), cedar/juniper (10 percent), white oaks (2 percent), and black walnut (2 percent) were other major species groups harvested (Table 7, Fig. 4).

- The production of ponderosa pine for industrial roundwood was down dramatically from 2006, from 1.42 million cubic feet to 404,000 cubic feet in 2009.

- The Eastern Forest Inventory Unit produced 3.5 million cubic feet of industrial roundwood, 87 percent of total State production; the remaining 13 percent was produced in the Western unit.

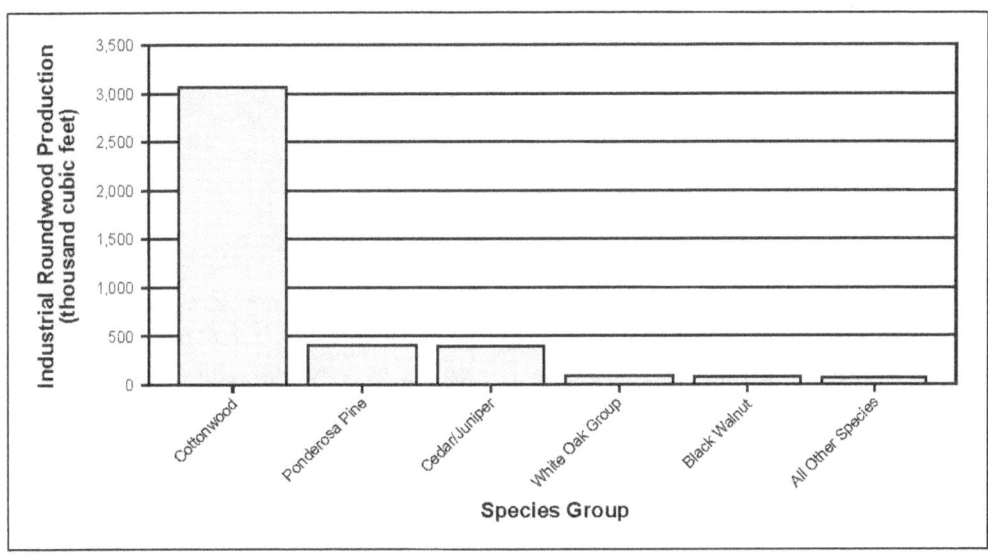

Figure 4.—Industrial roundwood production by species group, Nebraska, 2009.

- Harvesting saw logs accounted for 72 percent of the total industrial roundwood production. Excelsior/shaving mills were the second largest consumer of Nebraska's industrial roundwood production, consuming 20 percent of the total volume (Table 8, Fig. 5a–Fig. 5d).

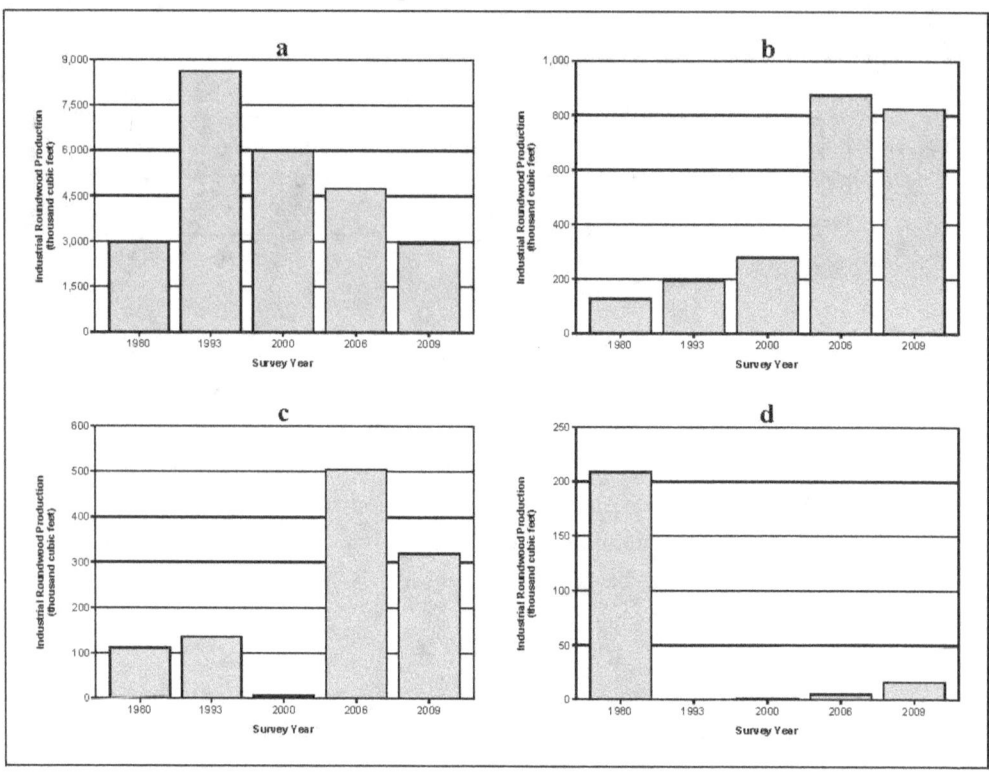

Figure 5.—Industrial roundwood production by survey year and (a) saw logs, (b) excelsior/shavings, (c) veneer logs, (d) posts and other products, Nebraska (Blyth et al. 1984, Hackett and Adams 1996, Reading and Adams 2002, Piva and Adams 2008).

## Saw Logs

- Receipts at Nebraska sawmills totaled 19.3 million board feet in 2009, a decrease of 16 percent from the 22.9 million board feet received in 2006 (Table 9).

- Saw log production decreased by 37 percent between 2006 and 2009, from 29.5 to 18.5 million board feet.

- Cottonwood accounted for 80 percent of the total volume of saw log production in Nebraska. Other important species groups in saw log production were ponderosa pine (11 percent of total), white oaks, and black walnut (3 percent of total each) (Fig. 6).

- Ponderosa pine saw log production dropped by 76 percent, from 8.2 million board feet in 2006 to 1.9 million board feet in 2009.

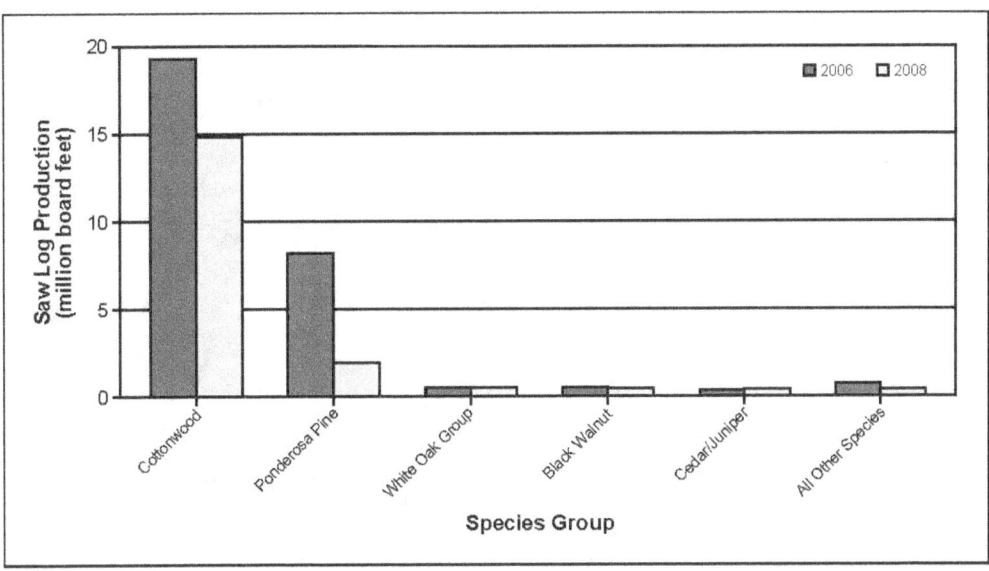

Figure 6.—Saw log production by species group, Nebraska, 2006 and 2009 (Piva and Adams 2008).

## Other Products

- Excelsior/shavings, at 823,000 cubic feet, was the second most harvested product in Nebraska for 2006. Cottonwood (56 percent of total), cedar/juniper (36 percent), and ponderosa pine (8 percent) were the only species groups that were harvested for excelsior/shavings.

- Veneer log harvests amounted to 319,000 cubic feet (1.4 million board feet). Cottonwood and black walnut were the only species harvested for veneer.

- Posts and other miscellaneous products made up the rest of Nebraska harvests in 2006. These products accounted for less than 1 percent of the total volume of industrial roundwood production.

## Timber Removals

- The harvest of industrial roundwood from Nebraska's forests in 2009 resulted in 5.6 million cubic feet of total wood material cut with 4.1 million cubic feet (73 percent) used for primary wood products and 1.5 million cubic feet (27 percent) left on the ground as harvest residues (Table 10, Fig. 7).

- Growing-stock sources, at 4.55 million cubic feet, was the largest component of removals for industrial roundwood production. Eighty-nine percent of the growing-stock removed was used for products, and the remaining 11 percent was left as logging residue. Sawtimber-size trees accounted for 98 percent of the growing-stock volume used for products.

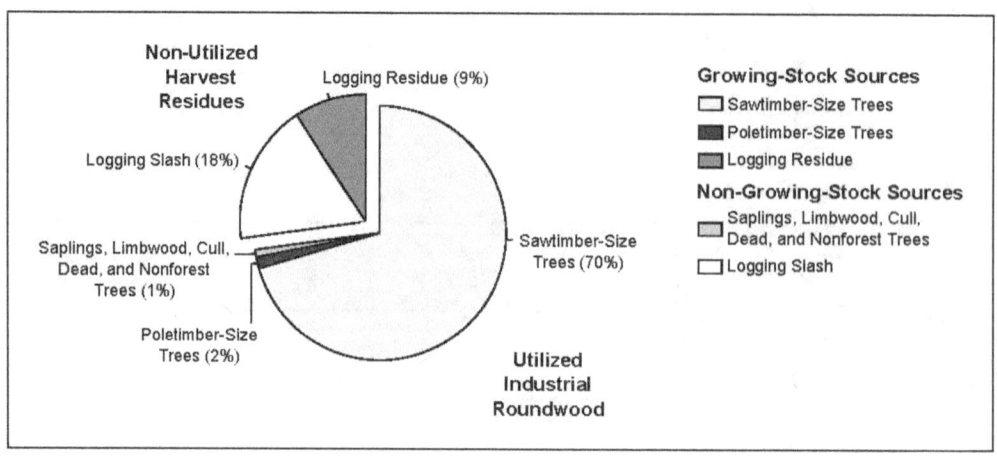

Figure 7.—Distribution of timber removals for industrial roundwood by source of material, Nebraska, 2009.

- Non-growing-stock sources of industrial roundwood production accounted for 1.06 million cubic feet of wood material removed. Five percent of this material was used for products; the remainder was left on the ground as logging slash. Seventy-two percent of the non-growing-stock material used for industrial roundwood came from cull trees; the rest of the volume used came from the limbs of growing-stock trees, saplings, dead trees, and nonforest trees.

- Eighty-seven percent of the total growing-stock material removed from Nebraska's timberland came from the Eastern Forest Inventory Unit, and the remaining 13 percent came from the Western unit (Table 11).

- More than 25 million board feet of sawtimber was removed from Nebraska's timberland. Cottonwood, ponderosa pine, and cedar/juniper accounted for 96 percent of the total sawtimber volume removed (Table 12).

- Ninety percent of the harvest residue in Nebraska was produced in the Eastern Forest Inventory Unit; the remainder was produced in the Western unit (Table 13).

## Harvest Intensity

- In 2009, there were nearly 1.5 million acres of forest land in Nebraska (Meneguzzo 2011). The net volume in live trees on forest land was 2 billion cubic feet. The 5.6 million cubic feet of total wood material removed due to harvesting (Table 10) was less than 1 percent of the total volume (trees at least 5 inches d.b.h.).

- Harvest intensity across the State was light; only five counties had more than 25 cubic feet of industrial roundwood production per acre of forest land (Fig. 8). Some counties in which primary wood-using mills reported receiving roundwood had 0 acres of forest land as estimated by the FIA inventory. Therefore, we were unable to calculate harvest intensity for those counties.

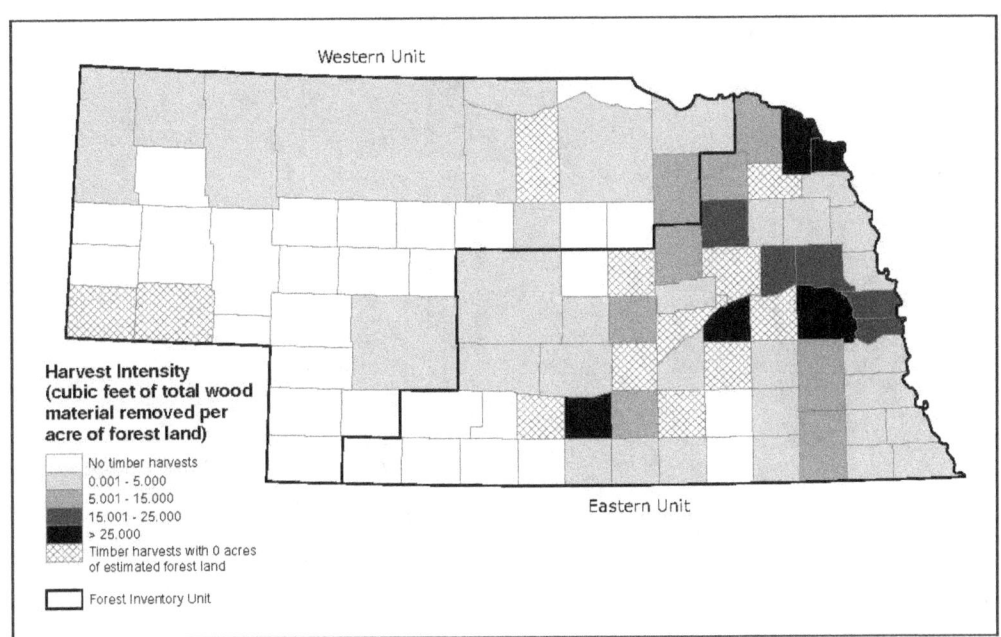

Figure 8.—Harvest intensity of industrial roundwood by county, Nebraska, 2009.

- The Eastern unit had the greater harvest intensity of the two Forest Inventory units at 7.14 cubic feet of wood material removed per acre of forest land. The Western unit had less than 1 cubic foot of wood material removed per acre.

## Primary Mill Residues

- In converting industrial roundwood into products, Nebraska's primary wood-using industries generated 68,000 green tons of coarse wood residue (slabs, edgings, and veneer cores), fine wood residues (sawdust and veneer clippings), and bark residue (Table 14, Fig. 9a and Fig. 9b).

- Thirty-nine percent of mill residues generated were used for mulch. Miscellaneous uses, such as livestock bedding or specialty products, consumed 19 percent of mill residues, while industrial and residential fuel, combined, accounted for 18 percent. Twenty-four percent of residues generated went unused (Fig. 10).

- The top disposal method of coarse wood residue and bark was mulch, at 37 percent and 55 percent of the totals, respectively. Industrial fuel was the top disposal method of fine wood residue at 32 percent of the total.

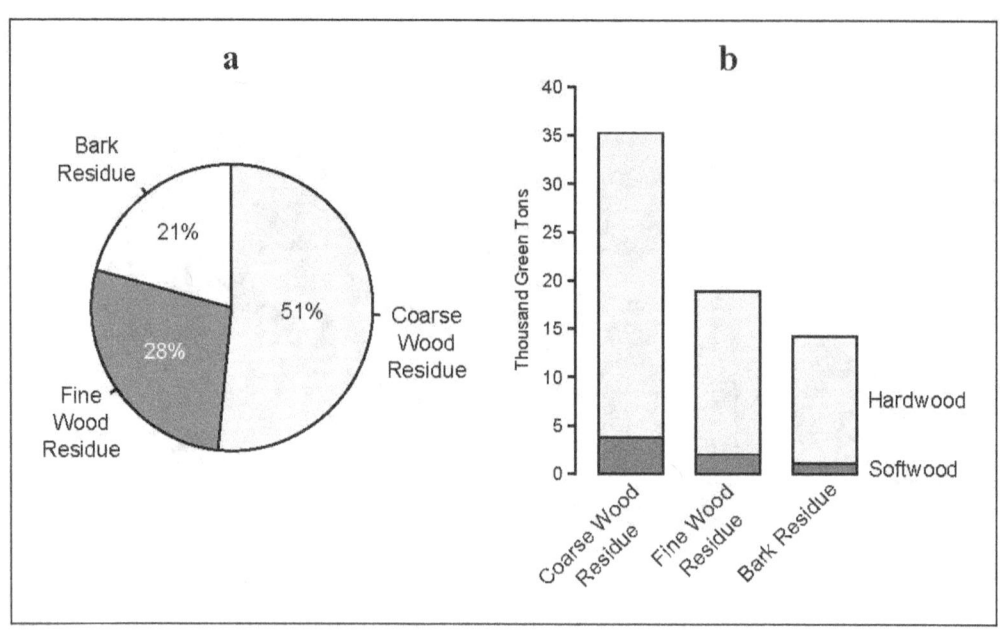

Figure 9.—Residues generated by primary wood-using mills by type of residue (a) and major species group (b), Nebraska, 2009.

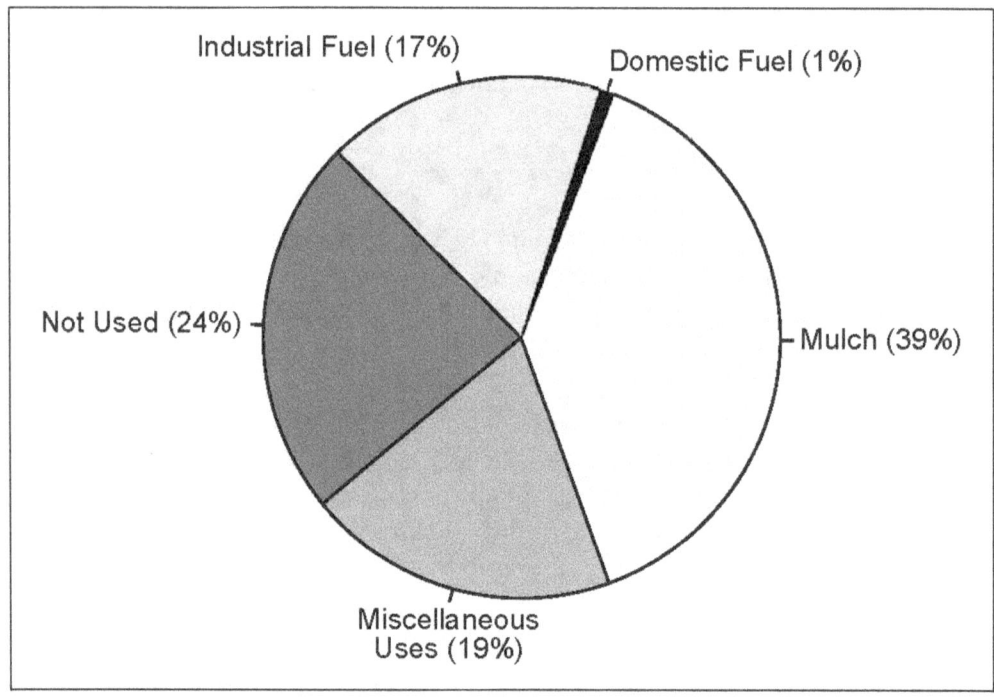

Figure 10.—Disposal of mill residue by product, Nebraska, 2009.

## ACKNOWLEDGMENTS

Special thanks are given to the primary wood-using firms for supplying information for this study and to the Nebraska Forest Service for its cooperation in canvassing survey respondents.

## LITERATURE CITED

Blyth, J.E.; Wardle, T.D.; Smith, W.B. 1984. **Primary forest products industry and timber use, Nebraska, 1980.** Resour. Bull. NC-80. St. Paul, MN: U.S. Department of Agriculture, Forest Service, North Central Forest Experiment Station. 11 p.

Hackett, R.L.; Adams, D.M. 1996. **Nebraska timber industry – an assessment of timber product output and use, 1993.** Resour. Bull. NC-177. St. Paul, MN: U.S. Department of Agriculture, Forest Service, North Central Forest Experiment Station. 35 p.

Meneguzzo, D.M. 2011. **Nebraska's forest resources, 2009.** Res. Note NRS-93. Newtown Square, PA: U.S. Department of Agriculture, Forest Service, Northern Research Station. 4 p.

Piva, R.J.; Adams, D.M. 2008. **Nebraska timber industry – an assessment of timber product output and use, 2006.** Resour. Bull. NRS-28. Newtown Square, PA: U.S. Department of Agriculture, Forest Service, Northern Research Station. 54 p.

Reading, W.H. IV; Adams, D.M. 2002. **Nebraska timber industry – an assessment of timber product output and use, 2000.** Resour. Bull. NC-208. St. Paul, MN: U.S. Department of Agriculture, Forest Service, North Central Research Station. 32 p.

U.S. Census Bureau. 2007. **2007 Economic Census, Nebraska – Manufacturing: Geographic Area Series: Industry Statistics for the States, Metropolitan and Micropolitan Statistical Areas, Counties, and Places: 2007.** Generated by Brian Walters using American FactFinder; <http://factfinder.census.gov>. [Accessed April 16, 2012].

# APPENDIX
## Definition of Terms

**Board foot.** Unit of measure for lumber cut from roundwood. One board foot is equivalent to a board that is 1 foot long, 1 foot wide, and 1 inch thick.

**Bolt.** A short log no more than 8 feet long, to be sawn for lumber, peeled or sliced for veneer, shaved for excelsior, or converted into shingles, cooperage stock, dimension stock, blocks, blanks, or other products.

**Central stem.** The portion of a tree between a 1-foot stump and the minimum 4.0-inch top diameter outside bark, or point where the central stem breaks into limbs.

**Coarse mill residue.** Wood residue suitable for chipping such as slabs, edgings, and veneer cores.

**Commercial species.** Tree species presently or prospectively suitable for industrial wood products. (Note: Excludes species of typically small size, poor form, or inferior quality such as hophornbeam, Osage-orange, and redbud.)

**Cull removals.** Net volume of rough and rotten trees plus the net volume in sections of the central stem of growing-stock trees that do not meet regional merchantability standards but are harvested for industrial roundwood products.

**Diameter at breast height (d.b.h.).** The outside bark diameter at 4.5 feet above the forest floor on the uphill side of the tree. For determining breast height, the forest floor includes the duff layer that may be present, but does not include unincorporated woody debris that may rise above the ground line.

**Doyle rule.** A simple log rule or formula for estimating the board-foot volume of logs based on a 4-inch slabbing allowance to square the log. This rule is used in the Eastern and Southern United States.

**Exports.** The volume of roundwood utilized by mills outside the state where the timber was harvested.

**Fine mill residue.** Wood residue not suitable for chipping, such as sawdust and veneer clippings.

**Forest land.** Land at least 10-percent stocked with trees of any size, or formerly having had such tree cover, and not currently developed for nonforest use. (Note: Stocking is measured by comparing specified standards with basal area and/or number of trees, age or size, and spacing.) The minimum area for classification of forest land is 1 acre. Roadside, streamside, and shelterbelt strips of timber must have a crown width of at least 120 feet to qualify as forest land. Unimproved roads and trails, streams or other bodies of water, or clearings in forest areas shall be classified as forest if less than 120 feet wide.

**Growing-stock removals.** The growing-stock volume removed from timberland by harvesting industrial roundwood products. (Note: Includes sawtimber removals, poletimber removals, and logging residues.)

**Growing-stock tree.** A live timberland tree of commercial species that meets specified standards of size, quality, and merchantability. (Note: Excludes rough, rotten, and dead trees.)

**Growing-stock volume.** Net volume of growing-stock trees 5.0 inches d.b.h. and larger, from 1 foot above the ground to a minimum 4.0-inch top diameter outside bark of the central stem or to the point where the central stem breaks into limbs.

**Hardwoods.** Dicotyledonous trees, usually broad-leaved and deciduous.

**Harvest residues.** The total net volume of unused portions of trees cut or killed by logging. (Note: Includes both logging residues and logging slash.)

**Industrial fuelwood.** A roundwood product, with or without bark, used to generate energy at manufacturing facilities and schools, correctional institutions, or electric generating plants.

**Imports.** The volume of roundwood delivered to a mill or group of mills in a specific state but harvested outside that state.

**Industrial roundwood exports.** The quantity of industrial roundwood harvested in a geographical area and transported to other geographical areas.

**Industrial roundwood imports.** The quantity of industrial roundwood received from other geographical areas.

**Industrial roundwood products.** Saw logs, pulpwood, veneer logs, poles, commercial posts, pilings, cooperage logs, particleboard bolts, shaving bolts, lath bolts, charcoal bolts, and chips from roundwood used for pulp or board products.

**Industrial roundwood production.** The quantity of industrial roundwood harvested in a geographic area plus all industrial roundwood exported to other geographical areas.

**Industrial roundwood receipts.** The quantity of industrial roundwood received by commercial mills in a geographic area plus all industrial roundwood imported from other geographical areas.

**Industrial roundwood retained.** The quantity of industrial roundwood harvested from and processed by commercial mills within the same geographical area.

**International ¼-inch rule.** A log rule or formula for estimating the board-foot volume of logs, allowing ½ inch of taper for each 4-foot length and assuming ¼ inch of kerf. This rule is used as the U.S. Forest Service standard log rule in the Eastern United States.

**Limbwood removals.** Net volume of all portions of a tree other than the central stem (including forks, large limbs, tops, and stumps) harvested for industrial roundwood products.

**Logging residue.** The net volume of unused portions of the merchantable central stem of growing-stock trees cut or killed by logging.

**Logging slash.** The net volume of unused portions of the unmerchantable (non-growing-stock) sections of trees cut or killed by logging.

**Merchantable sections.** Refers to sections of the central stem of growing-stock trees that meet either pulpwood or saw log specifications.

**Net volume.** Gross volume less deductions for rot, sweep, or other defects affecting use for roundwood products.

**Noncommercial species.** Trees species of typically small size, poor form, or inferior quality that normally do not develop into trees suitable for industrial roundwood products. Noncommercial species are listed in the volume tables as rough trees.

**Nonforest land.** Land that has never supported forests, and land formerly forested where use for timber management is precluded by development for other uses. (Note: Includes areas used for crops, active Christmas tree plantations, orchards, nurseries, improved pasture, residential areas, city parks, improved roads of any width and adjoining clearings, powerline clearings of any width, and 1- to 39.9-acre areas of water classified by the Bureau of the Census as land.) If intermingled in forest areas, unimproved roads and nonforest strips must be more than 120 feet wide and more than 1 acre to qualify as nonforest land.

**Nonforest land removals.** Net volume of trees on nonforest lands harvested for industrial roundwood products.

**Poletimber.** A growing-stock tree at least 5.0 inches d.b.h. but smaller than sawtimber size (9.0 inches d.b.h. for softwoods, 11.0 inches d.b.h. for hardwoods).

**Poletimber removals.** Net volume in the merchantable central stem of poletimber trees harvested for industrial roundwood products.

**Primary wood-using mills.** Mills receiving roundwood or chips from roundwood for processing into products such as lumber, veneer, and pulp.

**Primary wood-using mill residue.** Wood materials (coarse and fine) and bark generated at manufacturing plants that process industrial roundwood into principal products. These residues include wood products obtained incidental to production of principal products and wood materials not utilized for some product.

**Production.** The quantity of roundwood material harvested in a geographic area plus all roundwood material exported to other geographical areas.

**Receipts.** The quantity of roundwood material received by commercial mills in a geographic area plus all roundwood material imported from other geographical areas.

**Retained.** Roundwood volume harvested from and processed by mills within the same state.

**Rotten tree.** A tree that does not meet regional merchantability standards because of excessive unsound cull.

**Rough tree.** A tree that does not meet regional merchantability standards because of excessive sound cull (includes forks, sweep and crook, and large branches or knots), including noncommercial tree species.

**Roundwood.** Logs, bolts, or other round sections cut from trees (including chips from roundwood).

**Sapling.** A live tree between 1.0 and 5.0 inches d.b.h.

**Saw log portion.** That portion of the central stem of sawtimber trees between the stump and the saw log top.

**Saw log top.** The point on the central stem of sawtimber trees above which a saw log cannot be produced. The minimum saw log top is 7.0 inches diameter outside bark for softwoods and 9.0 inches diameter outside bark for hardwoods.

**Sawtimber removals.** As used in Table 10, sawtimber removals refers to the net volume in the merchantable central stem of sawtimber-size trees harvested for industrial roundwood products. (Note: includes the saw log and upper stem portions of sawtimber-size trees.) When referring to the sawtimber volume removed from timberland as in Table 12, sawtimber removals refers to the net volume in the saw log portion of sawtimber-size trees harvested for roundwood products or left on the ground as harvest residue, and is usually expressed in thousands of board feet (International ¼-inch rule).

**Sawtimber tree.** A growing-stock tree containing at least a 12-foot saw log or two noncontiguous saw logs 8 feet or longer, and meeting regional specifications for freedom from defect. Softwoods must be at least 9.0 inches d.b.h. and hardwoods must be at least 11.0 inches d.b.h.

**Sawtimber volume.** Net volume in the saw log portion of sawtimber trees.

**Softwoods.** Coniferous trees, usually evergreen, having needles or scale-like leaves.

**Timber product output.** The volume of roundwood products produced from an area's forests.

**Timberland.** Forest land that is producing, or is capable of producing, in excess of 20 cubic feet per acre per year of industrial roundwood products under natural conditions, is not withdrawn from timber utilization by statute or administrative regulation, and is not associated with urban or rural development.

**Tree.** A woody perennial plant, typically large, with a single well-defined stem carrying a more or less definite crown; sometimes defined as attaining a minimum diameter of 3 in. (7.6 cm) and a minimum height of 15 ft (4.6 m) at maturity. For FIA, any plant on the tree list in the current field manual is measured as a tree.

**Upper stem portion.** That portion of the central stem of sawtimber trees between the saw log top and the minimum top diameter of 4.0 inches outside bark, or to the point where the central stem breaks into limbs.

## Common and Scientific Names of Tree Species in Nebraska by TPO Species Group

**Softwoods**

Cedar/juniper

    Rocky Mountain juniper            *Juniperus scopulorum*

    Eastern redcedar                 *Juniperus virginiana*

Ponderosa pine                   *Pinus ponderosa*

White pine

    Eastern white pine               *Pinus strobus*

**Hardwoods**

Soft maple

    Boxelder                      *Acer negundo*

    Silver maple                  *Acer saccharinum*

Hickory

    Bitternut hickory                *Carya cordiformis*

    Shagbark hickory             *Carya ovata*

Hackberry                       *Celtis occidentalis*

Ash

    Green ash                    *Fraxinus pennsylvanica*

Black walnut                  *Juglans nigra*

American sycamore           *Platanus occidentalis*

Cottonwood

    Eastern cottonwood         *Populus deltoides*

    Plains cottonwood           *Populus deltoides ssp. Monilifera*

Black cherry                  *Prunus serotina*

Red oak group

    Northern red oak             *Quercus rubra*

    Black oak                    *Quercus velutina*

White oak group

    Bur oak                      *Quercus macrocarpa*

    Chinkapin oak                *Quercus muehlenbergii*

Basswood

    American basswood (Linden)     *Tilia americana*

Elm

    American elm                                *Ulmus Americana*

    Siberian elm                                  *Ulmus pumila*

    Slippery elm                                  *Ulmus rubra*

Other hardwoods

    Honeylocust                                  *Gleditsia triacanthos*

    Black locust                                  *Robinia pseudoacacia*

    Black willow                                  *Salix nigra*

    Kentucky coffeetree                        *Gymnocladus dioicus*

## Tables

Table 1.–Conversion factors from reported unit of measure to standard unit of measure (This table is in the Study Methods section.)

Table 2.–Number of active primary wood-using mills by mill type and survey year, Nebraska

Table 3.–Industrial roundwood receipts, in thousand cubic feet, by mill type, survey year, and softwoods and hardwoods, Nebraska

Table 4.–Industrial roundwood receipts, in thousand cubic feet, by species group and state of origin, Nebraska, 2009

Table 5.–Industrial roundwood production, in thousand cubic feet, by product, softwoods and hardwoods, and survey year, Nebraska

Table 6.–Industrial roundwood production, in thousand cubic feet, by species group and state of destination, Nebraska, 2009

Table 7.–Industrial roundwood production, in thousand cubic feet, by Forest Inventory Unit, county, and species group, Nebraska, 2009

Table 8.–Industrial roundwood production by Forest Inventory Unit, species group, and product, Nebraska, 2009

Table 9.–Saw log receipts and production, in thousand board feet, International ¼-inch rule, by species group, Nebraska, 2006 and 2009

Table 10.–Wood material harvested for industrial roundwood, in thousand cubic feet, by species group and source of material, Nebraska, 2009

Table 11.–Growing-stock removals from timberland for industrial roundwood, in thousand cubic feet, by Forest Inventory Unit, county, and species group, Nebraska, 2009

Table 12.–Sawtimber removals from timberland for industrial roundwood, in thousand board feet, International ¼-inch rule, by Forest Inventory Unit, county, and species group, Nebraska, 2009

Table 13.–Harvest residue generated by industrial roundwood harvesting, in thousand cubic feet, by Forest Inventory Unit, county, and species group, Nebraska, 2009

Table 14.–Disposition of residues produced at primary wood-using mills, in green tons, by Forest Inventory Unit, disposition, residue type, and softwoods and hardwoods, Nebraska, 2009

Table 2.–Number of active primary wood-using mills by mill type and survey year, Nebraska

| Mill type and mill size | Survey year | | | | | |
|---|---|---|---|---|---|---|
| | 1980[c] | 1993 | 2000 | 2006 | 2009 |
| Sawmills[a] | | | | | |
| 5,000 mbf or greater | -- | 2 | 2 | 2 | 2 |
| Between 1,000 and 4,999 mbf | 7 | 10 | 5 | 3 | 2 |
| Between 100 and 999 mbf | 35 | 8 | 6 | 10 | 8 |
| Less than 100 mbf | | 12 | 19 | 34 | 45 |
| Total | 42 | 32 | 32 | 49 | 57 |
| Veneer mills | -- | 1 | -- | 1 | 1 |
| Post, pole, piling mills | 2 | -- | -- | 2 | 3 |
| Other mills[b] | 2 | 2 | 2 | 2 | 1 |
| All mills | 46 | 35 | 34 | 54 | 62 |

[a] Annual lumber production in thousand board feet (mbf), International ¼-inch rule.

[b] Includes mills producing excelsior/shavings, cabin logs, etc.

[c] Numbers to categorize sawmills producing less than 1,000 mbf of lumber are unavailable for 1980.

Table 3.–Industrial roundwood receipts, in thousand cubic feet, by mill type, survey year, and softwoods and hardwoods, Nebraska

| | Survey year | | | | | 2006 - 2009 |
| | 1993 | 2000 | 2006 | 2009 | % change |
|---|---|---|---|---|---|
| **All Species** | | | | | |
| Saw mills | 6,504 | 4,414 | 3,560 | 2,986 | -16 |
| Post, pole, piling mills | -- | -- | 5 | 9 | 92 |
| Other mills[a] | 290 | 296 | 1,542 | 1,138 | -26 |
| Total | 6,794 | 4,711 | 5,106 | 4,133 | -19 |
| **Softwoods** | | | | | |
| Saw mills | 950 | 129 | 85 | 104 | 22 |
| Post, pole, piling mills | -- | -- | 1 | 8 | 567 |
| Other mills[a] | 119 | 279 | 681 | 362 | -47 |
| Total | 1,068 | 408 | 767 | 473 | -38 |
| **Hardwoods** | | | | | |
| Saw mills | 5,554 | 4,286 | 3,475 | 2,882 | -17 |
| Post, pole, piling mills | -- | -- | 3 | 1 | -67 |
| Other mills[a] | 172 | 17 | 861 | 776 | -10 |
| Total | 5,725 | 4,303 | 4,339 | 3,659 | -16 |

Columns and rows may not add to their totals due to rounding.

[a] Includes mills producing excelsior/shavings, cabin logs, etc.

Table 4.–Industrial roundwood receipts, in thousand cubic feet, by species group and state of origin, Nebraska, 2009

| Species group | Total | State of origin | | | | |
| --- | --- | --- | --- | --- | --- | --- |
| | | Iowa | Kansas | Missouri | Nebraska | South Dakota |
| **Softwoods** | | | | | | |
| Cedar/juniper | 383 | -- | -- | -- | 383 | -- |
| Ponderosa pine | 90 | -- | -- | -- | 90 | -- |
| White pine | 0 | -- | -- | -- | 0 | -- |
| Total | 473 | -- | -- | -- | 473 | -- |
| **Hardwoods** | | | | | | |
| Ash | 26 | 2 | -- | -- | 24 | -- |
| Black walnut | 38 | 8 | -- | 8 | 23 | 8 |
| Cottonwood | 3,443 | 376 | -- | -- | 3,059 | 8 |
| Elm | 18 | 2 | -- | -- | 17 | -- |
| Hackberry | 6 | 1 | -- | -- | 5 | -- |
| Hickory | 1 | -- | -- | 1 | -- | -- |
| Soft maple | 13 | 2 | -- | -- | 11 | -- |
| Red oak group | 3 | -- | 2 | -- | 1 | -- |
| White oak group | 106 | 12 | 5 | 2 | 86 | 0 |
| Other hardwoods | 6 | 1 | -- | -- | 5 | -- |
| Total | 3,659 | 404 | 7 | 11 | 3,230 | 8 |
| State total | 4,133 | 404 | 7 | 11 | 3,704 | 8 |

*All table cells without observations are indicated by --. Table value of 0 indicates the volume rounds to less than 1 thousand cubic feet. Columns and rows may not add to their totals due to rounding.*

Table 5.—Industrial roundwood production, in thousand cubic feet, by product, softwoods and hardwoods, and survey year, Nebraska

| Product | Survey year | | | | | % change from 2006 - 2009 |
|---|---|---|---|---|---|---|
| | 1980 | 1993 | 2000 | 2006 | 2009 | |
| **All species** | | | | | | |
| Saw logs | 2,967 | 8,625 | 5,995 | 4,742 | 2,930 | -38% |
| Veneer logs | 112 | 136 | 6 | 505 | 319 | -37% |
| Excelsior/shavings | 126 | 194 | 279 | 875 | 823 | -6% |
| Industrial fuelwood | -- | -- | 14 | 8 | -- | -- |
| Posts | 209 | -- | 0 | 5 | 9 | 92% |
| Other products[a] | -- | -- | -- | -- | 7 | -- |
| Total | 3,414 | 8,955 | 6,294 | 6,135 | 4,087 | -33% |
| **Softwoods** | | | | | | |
| Saw logs | 313 | 3,876 | 2,266 | 1,491 | 420 | -72% |
| Veneer logs | -- | -- | -- | -- | -- | -- |
| Excelsior/shavings | 106 | 119 | 279 | 703 | 362 | -48% |
| Industrial fuelwood | -- | -- | -- | -- | -- | -- |
| Posts | 88 | -- | 0 | 1 | 8 | 567% |
| Other products[a] | -- | -- | -- | -- | 7 | -- |
| Total | 507 | 3,995 | 2,545 | 2,195 | 797 | -64% |
| **Hardwoods** | | | | | | |
| Saw logs | 2,654 | 4,749 | 3,729 | 3,252 | 2,510 | -23% |
| Veneer logs | 112 | 136 | 6 | 505 | 319 | -37% |
| Excelsior/shavings | 20 | 75 | -- | 172 | 461 | 168% |
| Industrial fuelwood | -- | -- | 14 | 8 | -- | -- |
| Posts | 121 | -- | -- | 3 | 1 | -67% |
| Other products[a] | -- | -- | -- | -- | -- | -- |
| Total | 2,907 | 4,960 | 3,750 | 3,940 | 3,291 | -16% |

*All table cells without observations are indicated by -- . Table value of 0 indicates the volume rounds to less than 1 thousand cubic feet. Columns and rows may not add to their totals due to rounding.*

a Includes cabin logs and other miscellaneous products.

Table 6.—Industrial roundwood production, in thousand cubic feet, by species group and state of destination, Nebraska, 2009

| Species group | Total | State of destination | | | | | |
| --- | --- | --- | --- | --- | --- | --- | --- |
| | | Iowa | Missouri | Nebraska | South Dakota | Wyoming | Other Countries |
| Softwoods | | | | | | | |
| Cedar/juniper | 393 | -- | -- | 383 | 9 | 0 | -- |
| Ponderosa pine | 404 | -- | -- | 90 | 2 | 312 | -- |
| White pine | 0 | -- | -- | 0 | -- | -- | -- |
| Total | 797 | -- | -- | 473 | 12 | 312 | -- |
| Hardwoods | | | | | | | |
| Ash | 24 | -- | -- | 24 | -- | -- | -- |
| Black walnut | 76 | 44 | 4 | 23 | -- | 1 | 4 |
| Cottonwood | 3,063 | -- | 4 | 3,059 | -- | -- | -- |
| Elm | 17 | -- | -- | 17 | -- | -- | -- |
| Hackberry | 5 | -- | -- | 5 | -- | -- | -- |
| Soft maple | 12 | -- | 1 | 11 | -- | -- | -- |
| Red oak group | 3 | -- | 1 | 1 | -- | -- | -- |
| White oak group | 86 | -- | 0 | 86 | -- | -- | -- |
| Sycamore | 0 | -- | 0 | -- | -- | -- | -- |
| Other hardwoods | 5 | -- | -- | 5 | -- | -- | -- |
| Total | 3,291 | 44 | 11 | 3,230 | -- | 1 | -- |
| State total | 4,087 | 44 | 11 | 3,704 | 12 | 313 | 4 |

*All table cells without observations are indicated by -- . Table value of 0 indicates the volume rounds to less than 1 thousand cubic feet. Columns and rows may not add to their totals due to rounding.*

Table 7.—Industrial roundwood production, in thousand cubic feet, by Forest Inventory Unit, county, and species group, Nebraska, 2009

| Forest Inventory Unit and county | All species | Softwoods | | | | Hardwoods | | |
| | | Cedar/ juniper | Ponderosa pine | White pine | Total softwoods | Ash | Black walnut | Cotton- wood |
|---|---|---|---|---|---|---|---|---|
| **Eastern Unit** | | | | | | | | |
| Adams | 61 | -- | -- | -- | -- | 2 | -- | 53 |
| Boone | 23 | 1 | -- | -- | 1 | -- | -- | 22 |
| Buffalo | 64 | 0 | -- | -- | 0 | 2 | 0 | 55 |
| Burt | 6 | -- | -- | -- | -- | -- | -- | 6 |
| Butler | 7 | 0 | -- | -- | 0 | -- | 0 | 6 |
| Cass | 0 | -- | -- | -- | -- | -- | 0 | -- |
| Cedar | 128 | 0 | -- | -- | 0 | -- | -- | 128 |
| Clay | 0 | -- | -- | -- | -- | -- | -- | -- |
| Colfax | 171 | 33 | -- | -- | 33 | -- | -- | 138 |
| Cuming | 17 | 1 | 0 | -- | 1 | 0 | -- | 15 |
| Custer | 0 | 0 | -- | -- | 0 | -- | 0 | -- |
| Dakota | 322 | -- | -- | -- | -- | -- | 0 | 321 |
| Dawson | 1 | 1 | -- | -- | 1 | -- | -- | -- |
| Dixon | 162 | 0 | -- | -- | 0 | -- | 0 | 161 |
| Dodge | 187 | 33 | -- | 0 | 33 | 1 | 0 | 145 |
| Douglas | 175 | -- | -- | -- | -- | 2 | -- | 158 |
| Franklin | 61 | -- | -- | -- | -- | 2 | -- | 53 |
| Gage | 13 | 0 | -- | -- | 0 | 0 | 3 | 4 |
| Greeley | 66 | 33 | -- | -- | 33 | -- | -- | 33 |
| Hall | 62 | 1 | -- | -- | 1 | 2 | -- | 53 |
| Hamilton | 1 | -- | -- | -- | -- | -- | 1 | -- |

Table 7.—Continued

| Forest Inventory Unit and county | All species | Softwoods | | | | Hardwoods | | |
|---|---|---|---|---|---|---|---|---|
| | | Cedar/ juniper | Ponderosa pine | White pine | Total softwoods | Ash | Black walnut | Cotton- wood |
| Howard | 66 | 33 | -- | -- | 33 | -- | -- | 33 |
| Jefferson | 5 | 1 | -- | -- | 1 | -- | 4 | -- |
| Johnson | 0 | -- | -- | -- | -- | -- | -- | -- |
| Kearney | 61 | -- | -- | -- | -- | 2 | -- | 53 |
| Lancaster | 88 | -- | -- | -- | -- | 1 | 1 | 79 |
| Madison | 80 | -- | -- | -- | -- | -- | -- | 80 |
| Merrick | 139 | 71 | -- | -- | 71 | 2 | -- | 66 |
| Nance | 101 | 35 | -- | -- | 35 | -- | -- | 66 |
| Nemaha | 10 | 0 | -- | -- | 0 | -- | 9 | 0 |
| Nuckolls | 0 | -- | -- | -- | -- | -- | -- | -- |
| Otoe | 7 | -- | -- | -- | -- | -- | 7 | -- |
| Pawnee | 4 | 0 | -- | -- | 0 | -- | 2 | -- |
| Phelps | 0 | 0 | -- | -- | 0 | -- | -- | -- |
| Pierce | 64 | -- | -- | -- | -- | -- | -- | 64 |
| Platte | 116 | 34 | -- | -- | 34 | -- | -- | 82 |
| Polk | 117 | 36 | -- | -- | 36 | 0 | 0 | 79 |
| Richardson | 37 | -- | -- | -- | -- | 0 | 27 | 4 |
| Saline | 13 | -- | -- | -- | -- | 0 | 2 | 4 |
| Sarpy | 175 | -- | -- | -- | -- | 2 | -- | 158 |
| Saunders | 690 | 0 | -- | -- | 0 | 2 | 0 | 672 |
| Seward | 8 | 1 | -- | -- | 1 | 1 | 3 | 0 |
| Sherman | 6 | 4 | 1 | -- | 6 | -- | -- | -- |

Table 7.—Continued

| Forest Inventory Unit and county | Softwoods | | | | | Hardwoods | | |
|---|---|---|---|---|---|---|---|---|
| | All species | Cedar/ juniper | Ponderosa pine | White pine | Total softwoods | Ash | Black walnut | Cotton- wood |
| Stanton | 29 | -- | -- | -- | -- | -- | -- | 29 |
| Thurston | 7 | -- | -- | -- | -- | -- | 7 | -- |
| Washington | 5 | -- | -- | -- | -- | -- | 5 | -- |
| Wayne | 112 | 0 | -- | -- | 0 | -- | -- | 112 |
| Webster | 62 | 0 | -- | -- | 0 | 2 | 0 | 53 |
| York | 13 | 5 | -- | -- | 5 | 1 | 1 | 6 |
| Total | 3,542 | 326 | 2 | 0 | 328 | 22 | 74 | 2,991 |
| **Western Unit** | | | | | | | | |
| Antelope | 55 | 1 | 0 | -- | 1 | 0 | 0 | 53 |
| Brown | 16 | 16 | -- | -- | 16 | -- | -- | -- |
| Cherry | 18 | 7 | 10 | -- | 17 | 0 | 0 | 0 |
| Cheyenne | 1 | -- | -- | -- | -- | -- | -- | -- |
| Dawes | 162 | 1 | 161 | -- | 162 | -- | -- | -- |
| Holt | 2 | 2 | -- | -- | 2 | -- | -- | -- |
| Keya Paha | 94 | 19 | 74 | -- | 93 | 0 | 0 | -- |
| Kimball | 2 | -- | -- | -- | -- | 0 | -- | 1 |
| Knox | 24 | 7 | -- | -- | 7 | -- | 0 | 17 |
| Lincoln | 10 | 8 | 0 | -- | 9 | 0 | 0 | -- |
| Loup | 1 | 1 | -- | -- | 1 | -- | -- | -- |
| Rock | 5 | 5 | -- | -- | 5 | -- | -- | -- |
| Sheridan | 1 | -- | 1 | -- | 1 | -- | -- | -- |
| Sioux | 157 | 0 | 155 | -- | 156 | -- | 1 | -- |
| Total | 546 | 67 | 402 | -- | 469 | 1 | 2 | 71 |

Table 7.—Continued

| Forest Inventory Unit and county | Hardwoods | | | | | | | |
|---|---|---|---|---|---|---|---|---|
| | Elm | Hackberry | Soft maple | Red oak group | White oak group | Sycamore | Other hardwoods | Total hardwoods |
| **Eastern Unit** | | | | | | | | |
| Adams | 1 | -- | -- | -- | 5 | -- | -- | 61 |
| Boone | -- | -- | -- | -- | -- | -- | -- | 22 |
| Buffalo | 2 | -- | -- | -- | 5 | -- | -- | 64 |
| Burt | -- | -- | -- | -- | -- | -- | -- | 6 |
| Butler | -- | -- | -- | -- | 0 | -- | -- | 6 |
| Cass | -- | -- | -- | -- | -- | -- | -- | 0 |
| Cedar | -- | -- | -- | -- | -- | -- | -- | 128 |
| Clay | -- | -- | -- | -- | 0 | -- | -- | 0 |
| Colfax | -- | -- | -- | -- | -- | -- | -- | 138 |
| Cuming | 0 | 0 | -- | -- | -- | -- | 0 | 16 |
| Custer | -- | -- | -- | -- | -- | -- | -- | 0 |
| Dakota | -- | -- | -- | -- | 0 | -- | -- | 322 |
| Dawson | -- | -- | -- | -- | -- | -- | -- | -- |
| Dixon | -- | -- | -- | -- | -- | -- | -- | 162 |
| Dodge | 1 | 0 | 1 | 0 | 5 | -- | 0 | 154 |
| Douglas | 2 | 1 | 2 | 1 | 10 | -- | 1 | 175 |
| Franklin | 2 | -- | -- | -- | 5 | -- | -- | 61 |
| Gage | 0 | 0 | 1 | -- | 3 | -- | -- | 12 |
| Greeley | -- | -- | -- | -- | -- | -- | -- | 33 |
| Hall | 2 | -- | -- | -- | 5 | -- | -- | 61 |
| Hamilton | -- | -- | -- | -- | -- | -- | -- | 1 |
| Howard | -- | -- | -- | -- | -- | -- | -- | 33 |

Table 7.—Continued

| Forest Inventory Unit and county | Hardwoods | | | | | | | Total hardwoods |
|---|---|---|---|---|---|---|---|---|
| | Elm | Hackberry | Soft maple | Red oak group | White oak group | Sycamore | Other hardwoods | |
| Jefferson | -- | -- | -- | -- | 0 | -- | -- | 4 |
| Johnson | -- | -- | -- | -- | -- | -- | 0 | 0 |
| Kearney | 1 | -- | -- | -- | 5 | -- | -- | 61 |
| Lancaster | 1 | 0 | 1 | -- | 5 | -- | 0 | 88 |
| Madison | -- | -- | -- | -- | -- | -- | -- | 80 |
| Merrick | -- | -- | -- | -- | 1 | -- | -- | 68 |
| Nance | -- | -- | -- | -- | -- | -- | -- | 66 |
| Nemaha | -- | -- | -- | 0 | -- | -- | 0 | 10 |
| Nuckolls | -- | -- | -- | -- | 0 | -- | -- | 0 |
| Otoe | -- | -- | -- | -- | -- | -- | -- | 7 |
| Pawnee | -- | -- | -- | -- | 1 | -- | 0 | 4 |
| Phelps | -- | -- | -- | -- | -- | -- | -- | -- |
| Pierce | -- | -- | -- | -- | -- | -- | -- | 64 |
| Platte | -- | -- | -- | -- | -- | -- | -- | 82 |
| Polk | 0 | -- | -- | -- | -- | -- | -- | 80 |
| Richardson | -- | -- | 1 | 1 | 3 | 0 | -- | 37 |
| Saline | 0 | -- | 2 | -- | 4 | -- | -- | 13 |
| Sarpy | 2 | 1 | 2 | -- | 10 | -- | 1 | 175 |
| Saunders | 2 | 1 | 2 | -- | 10 | -- | 1 | 690 |
| Seward | 0 | 0 | 0 | -- | 1 | -- | -- | 6 |
| Sherman | -- | -- | -- | -- | -- | -- | -- | -- |
| Stanton | -- | -- | -- | -- | -- | -- | -- | 29 |
| Thurston | -- | -- | -- | -- | -- | -- | -- | 7 |

Table 7.—Continued

| Forest Inventory Unit and county | | Hardwoods | | | | | | |
|---|---|---|---|---|---|---|---|---|
| | Elm | Hackberry | Soft maple | Red oak group | White oak group | Sycamore | Other hardwoods | Total hardwoods |
| Washington | -- | -- | -- | -- | 0 | -- | -- | 5 |
| Wayne | -- | -- | -- | -- | 0 | -- | -- | 112 |
| Webster | 2 | 0 | 0 | -- | 5 | -- | 0 | 62 |
| York | -- | -- | -- | -- | 1 | -- | -- | 8 |
| Total | 16 | 5 | 12 | 3 | 85 | 0 | 5 | 3,214 |
| **Western Unit** | | | | | | | | |
| Antelope | -- | -- | -- | -- | 0 | -- | -- | 54 |
| Brown | -- | -- | -- | -- | -- | -- | 0 | 0 |
| Cherry | -- | -- | -- | -- | 0 | -- | -- | 1 |
| Cheyenne | 0 | -- | -- | -- | -- | -- | -- | 1 |
| Dawes | -- | -- | -- | -- | -- | -- | -- | -- |
| Holt | -- | -- | -- | -- | -- | -- | -- | -- |
| Keya Paha | -- | -- | -- | -- | 0 | -- | -- | 1 |
| Kimball | 0 | -- | -- | -- | -- | -- | -- | 2 |
| Knox | -- | -- | -- | -- | -- | -- | -- | 17 |
| Lincoln | -- | 0 | -- | -- | -- | -- | -- | 1 |
| Loup | -- | -- | -- | -- | -- | -- | -- | -- |
| Rock | -- | -- | -- | -- | -- | -- | -- | -- |
| Sheridan | -- | -- | -- | -- | -- | -- | -- | -- |
| Sioux | -- | -- | -- | -- | -- | -- | -- | 1 |
| Total | 1 | 0 | -- | -- | 1 | -- | 0 | 77 |
| State total | 17 | 5 | 12 | 3 | 86 | 0 | 5 | 3,291 |

All table cells without observations are indicated by --. Table value of 0 indicates the volume rounds to less than 1 thousand cubic feet. Columns and rows may not add to their totals due to rounding.

Table 8.–Industrial roundwood production by Forest Inventory Unit, species group, and product, Nebraska, 2009

ALL UNITS

| Species group | All products | Saw logs | | Veneer logs | | Excelsior/ shavings | Posts | | Other products[a] |
|---|---|---|---|---|---|---|---|---|---|
| | MCF[b] | MBF[c] | MCF[b] | MBF[c] | MCF[b] | MCF[b] | M pieces[d] | MCF[b] | MCF[b] |
| **Softwoods** | | | | | | | | | |
| Cedar/juniper | 393 | 385 | 82 | -- | -- | 296 | 10 | 8 | 7 |
| Ponderosa pine | 404 | 1,944 | 338 | -- | -- | 66 | -- | -- | -- |
| White pine | 0 | 0 | 0 | -- | -- | -- | -- | -- | -- |
| Total | 797 | 2,330 | 420 | -- | -- | 362 | 10 | 8 | 7 |
| **Hardwoods** | | | | | | | | | |
| Ash | 24 | 139 | 24 | -- | -- | -- | -- | -- | -- |
| Black walnut | 76 | 472 | 72 | 28 | 4 | -- | -- | -- | -- |
| Cottonwood | 3,063 | 14,820 | 2,287 | 1,378 | 315 | 461 | -- | -- | -- |
| Elm | 17 | 105 | 17 | -- | -- | -- | -- | -- | -- |
| Hackberry | 5 | 33 | 5 | -- | -- | -- | -- | -- | -- |
| Soft maple | 12 | 74 | 12 | -- | -- | -- | -- | -- | -- |
| Red oak group | 3 | 15 | 3 | -- | -- | -- | -- | -- | -- |
| White oak group | 86 | 482 | 86 | -- | -- | -- | -- | -- | -- |
| Sycamore | 0 | 3 | 0 | -- | -- | -- | -- | -- | -- |
| Other hardwoods | 5 | 25 | 4 | -- | -- | -- | 2 | 1 | -- |
| Total | 3,291 | 16,168 | 2,510 | 1,406 | 319 | 461 | 2 | 1 | -- |
| State total | 4,087 | 18,498 | 2,930 | 1,406 | 319 | 823 | 12 | 9 | 7 |

Table 8.—Continued

EASTERN UNIT

|  | All products | Saw logs | | Veneer logs | | Excelsior/ shavings | Posts | | Other products[a] |
|---|---|---|---|---|---|---|---|---|---|
| Species group | MCF[b] | MBF[c] | MCF[b] | MBF[c] | MCF[b] | MCF[b] | M pieces[d] | MCF[b] | MCF[b] |
| **Softwoods** | | | | | | | | | |
| Cedar/juniper | 326 | 117 | 25 | -- | -- | 296 | 6 | 5 | 0 |
| Ponderosa pine | 2 | 10 | 2 | -- | -- | -- | -- | -- | -- |
| White pine | 0 | 0 | 0 | -- | -- | -- | -- | -- | -- |
| Total | 328 | 127 | 27 | -- | -- | 296 | 6 | 5 | 0 |
| **Hardwoods** | | | | | | | | | |
| Ash | 22 | 131 | 22 | -- | -- | -- | -- | -- | -- |
| Black walnut | 74 | 456 | 70 | 28 | 4 | -- | -- | -- | -- |
| Cottonwood | 2,991 | 14,358 | 2,215 | 1,378 | 315 | 461 | -- | -- | -- |
| Elm | 16 | 101 | 16 | -- | -- | -- | -- | -- | -- |
| Hackberry | 5 | 30 | 5 | -- | -- | -- | -- | -- | -- |
| Soft maple | 12 | 74 | 12 | -- | -- | -- | -- | -- | -- |
| Red oak group | 3 | 15 | 3 | -- | -- | -- | -- | -- | -- |
| White oak group | 85 | 478 | 85 | -- | -- | -- | -- | -- | -- |
| Sycamore | 0 | 3 | 0 | -- | -- | -- | -- | -- | -- |
| Other hardwoods | 5 | 24 | 4 | -- | -- | -- | 2 | 1 | -- |
| Total | 3,214 | 15,670 | 2,433 | 1,406 | 319 | 461 | 2 | 1 | -- |
| Unit total | 3,542 | 15,797 | 2,459 | 1,406 | 319 | 757 | 8 | 6 | 0 |

Table 8.—Continued

WESTERN UNIT

| | All products | Saw logs | | Veneer logs | | Excelsior/ shavings | Posts | | Other products[a] |
|---|---|---|---|---|---|---|---|---|---|
| Species group | MCF[b] | MBF[c] | MCF[b] | MBF[c] | MCF[b] | MCF[b] | M pieces[d] | MCF[b] | MCF[b] |
| **Softwoods** | | | | | | | | | |
| Cedar/juniper | 67 | 268 | 57 | -- | -- | -- | 4 | 3 | 7 |
| Ponderosa pine | 402 | 1,935 | 336 | -- | -- | 66 | -- | -- | -- |
| Total | 469 | 2,203 | 393 | -- | -- | 66 | 4 | 3 | 7 |
| **Hardwoods** | -- | -- | -- | -- | -- | -- | -- | -- | -- |
| Ash | 1 | 8 | 1 | -- | -- | -- | -- | -- | -- |
| Black walnut | 2 | 16 | 2 | -- | -- | -- | -- | -- | -- |
| Cottonwood | 71 | 462 | 71 | -- | -- | -- | -- | -- | -- |
| Elm | 1 | 4 | 1 | -- | -- | -- | -- | -- | -- |
| Hackberry | 0 | 2 | 0 | -- | -- | -- | -- | -- | -- |
| White oak group | 1 | 4 | 1 | -- | -- | -- | -- | -- | -- |
| Other hardwoods | 0 | 2 | 0 | -- | -- | -- | -- | -- | -- |
| Total | 77 | 498 | 77 | -- | -- | -- | -- | -- | -- |
| Unit total | 546 | 2,701 | 470 | -- | -- | 66 | 4 | 3 | 7 |

All table cells without observations are indicated by -- . Table value of 0 indicates the volume rounds to less than 1 unit of measure. Columns and rows may not add to their totals due to rounding.

[a] Includes cabin logs and other miscellaneous products.

[b] Thousand cubic feet.

[c] Thousand board feet, International ¼-inch rule.

[d] Thousand pieces.

Table 9.—Saw log receipts and production, in thousand board feet, International ¼-inch rule, by species group, Nebraska, 2006 and 2009

| Species group | Receipts | | | Production | | |
|---|---|---|---|---|---|---|
| | 2006 | 2009 | Percent change | 2006 | 2009 | Percent change |
| **Softwoods** | | | | | | |
| Cedar/juniper | 305 | 372 | 22% | 322 | 385 | 20% |
| Ponderosa pine | 100 | 139 | 39% | 8,174 | 1,944 | -76% |
| White pine | -- | 0 | -- | -- | 0 | -- |
| Spruce | 13 | -- | -- | 13 | -- | -73% |
| Total | 418 | 511 | 22% | 8,508 | 2,330 | -73% |
| **Hardwoods** | | | | | | |
| Ash | 94 | 150 | 60% | 103 | 139 | 35% |
| Basswood | 141 | -- | -- | 151 | -- | -- |
| Black walnut | 304 | 216 | -29% | 499 | 472 | -5% |
| Cottonwood | 20,857 | 17,501 | -16% | 19,259 | 14,820 | -23% |
| Elm | 142 | 116 | -18% | 142 | 105 | -26% |
| Hackberry | 160 | 38 | -76% | 105 | 33 | -69% |
| Hickory | -- | 6 | -- | -- | -- | -- |
| Hard maple | 3 | -- | -- | 3 | -- | -- |
| Soft maple | 174 | 80 | -54% | 133 | 74 | -45% |
| Red oak group | 45 | 16 | -64% | 63 | 15 | -76% |
| White oak group | 550 | 592 | 8% | 492 | 482 | -2% |
| Sycamore | 1 | -- | -- | 11 | 3 | -71% |
| Other hardwoods | 1 | 31 | 6103% | 1 | 25 | 4999% |
| Total | 22,472 | 18,747 | -17% | 20,962 | 16,168 | -23% |
| State total | 22,890 | 19,259 | -16% | 29,470 | 18,498 | -37% |

*All table cells without observations are indicated by --. Table value of 0 indicates the volume rounds to less than 1 thousand board feet. Columns and rows may not add to their totals due to rounding.*

Table 10.—Wood material harvested for industrial roundwood, in thousand cubic feet, by species group and source of material, Nebraska, 2009[a]

SOURCE OF MATERIAL

| Species group | Growing stock | | | | Non-growing stock | | | | | | | Total wood material used | Total wood material not used | Total wood harvested |
| | Used for products | | Logging residue (not used) | Total growing stock | Used for products | | | | Non-forest trees | Logging slash (not used) | Total non-growing stock | | | |
| | Saw-timber | Pole-timber | | | Limb-wood | Saplings | Cull trees | Dead trees | | | | | | |
|---|---|---|---|---|---|---|---|---|---|---|---|---|---|---|
| **Softwoods** | | | | | | | | | | | | | | |
| Cedar/juniper | 359.3 | 30.6 | 27.5 | 417.4 | -- | 2.0 | 0.7 | 0.4 | -- | 38.6 | 41.7 | 393.0 | 66.1 | 459.1 |
| Ponderosa pine | 397.2 | 6.0 | 42.2 | 445.4 | -- | -- | 0.4 | -- | -- | 53.9 | 54.3 | 403.6 | 96.0 | 499.6 |
| White pine | 0.0 | -- | 0.0 | 0.1 | -- | -- | 0.0 | -- | -- | 0.0 | 0.0 | 0.0 | 0.0 | 0.1 |
| Total | 756.6 | 36.6 | 69.6 | 862.8 | -- | 2.0 | 1.0 | 0.4 | -- | 92.5 | 96.0 | 796.6 | 162.1 | 958.8 |
| **Hardwoods** | | | | | | | | | | | | | | |
| Ash | 21.5 | -- | 8.9 | 30.4 | 0.6 | -- | 1.7 | -- | -- | 8.2 | 10.4 | 23.8 | 17.1 | 40.9 |
| Black walnut | 63.8 | -- | 6.0 | 69.8 | 1.3 | -- | 1.9 | -- | 9.2 | 19.3 | 31.7 | 76.2 | 25.3 | 101.5 |
| Cottonwood | 3,020.9 | 41.9 | 412.1 | 3,475.0 | -- | -- | -- | -- | -- | 850.1 | 850.1 | 3,062.8 | 1,262.3 | 4,325.1 |
| Elm | 14.4 | -- | 1.6 | 16.0 | -- | -- | 1.8 | 0.5 | -- | 5.0 | 7.2 | 16.7 | 6.5 | 23.2 |
| Hackberry | 4.5 | -- | 0.5 | 5.0 | -- | -- | 0.6 | 0.1 | -- | 1.5 | 2.2 | 5.2 | 2.0 | 7.2 |
| Soft maple | 10.1 | -- | 1.1 | 11.2 | -- | -- | 1.3 | 0.3 | -- | 3.5 | 5.1 | 11.7 | 4.6 | 16.3 |
| Red oak group | 1.7 | 0.1 | 0.5 | 2.3 | 0.0 | -- | 0.9 | -- | -- | 0.7 | 1.6 | 2.7 | 1.2 | 3.9 |
| White oak group | 54.6 | 3.0 | 17.7 | 75.3 | 0.0 | -- | 28.4 | -- | -- | 22.0 | 50.5 | 86.1 | 39.7 | 125.8 |
| Sycamore | 0.4 | -- | 0.0 | 0.5 | -- | -- | 0.1 | 0.0 | -- | 0.1 | 0.2 | 0.5 | 0.2 | 0.7 |
| Other hardwoods | 4.0 | 0.2 | 0.4 | 4.7 | 0.0 | 0.0 | 0.6 | 0.1 | 0.1 | 1.2 | 2.1 | 5.2 | 1.6 | 6.8 |
| Total | 3,195.9 | 45.2 | 449.0 | 3,690.1 | 2.0 | 2.0 | 37.2 | 1.1 | 9.3 | 911.6 | 961.2 | 3,290.8 | 1,360.6 | 4,651.4 |
| State total | 3,952.5 | 81.8 | 518.6 | 4,552.9 | 2.0 | 2.1 | 38.2 | 1.5 | 9.3 | 1,004.1 | 1,057.2 | 4,087.4 | 1,522.7 | 5,610.1 |

*All table cells without observations are indicated by --. Table value of 0 indicates the volume rounds to less than 0.1 thousand cubic feet. Columns and rows may not add to their totals due to rounding.*

[a] Based on factors obtained from regional utilization studies.

Table 11.—Growing-stock removals from timberland for industrial roundwood, in thousand cubic feet, by Forest Inventory Unit, county, and species group, Nebraska, 2009

| Forest Inventory Unit and county | All species | Softwoods | | | | Hardwoods | | |
|---|---|---|---|---|---|---|---|---|
| | | Cedar/ juniper | Ponderosa pine | White pine | Total softwoods | Ash | Black walnut | Cotton- wood |
| **Eastern Unit** | | | | | | | | |
| Adams | 69 | -- | -- | -- | -- | 2 | -- | 61 |
| Boone | 26 | 1 | -- | -- | 1 | -- | -- | 25 |
| Buffalo | 72 | 0 | -- | -- | 0 | 2 | 0 | 63 |
| Burt | 7 | -- | -- | -- | -- | -- | -- | 7 |
| Butler | 7 | 0 | -- | -- | 0 | 0 | 0 | 6 |
| Cass | 0 | -- | -- | -- | -- | 0 | 0 | -- |
| Cedar | 147 | 0 | -- | -- | 0 | -- | -- | 147 |
| Clay | 0 | -- | -- | -- | -- | -- | -- | -- |
| Colfax | 188 | 36 | -- | -- | 36 | -- | -- | 153 |
| Cuming | 20 | 1 | 1 | -- | 1 | 1 | -- | 17 |
| Custer | 0 | 0 | -- | -- | 0 | -- | 0 | -- |
| Dakota | 371 | -- | -- | -- | -- | -- | 0 | 370 |
| Dawson | 1 | 1 | -- | -- | 1 | -- | -- | -- |
| Dixon | 186 | 0 | -- | -- | 0 | -- | 0 | 186 |
| Dodge | 208 | 36 | -- | 0 | 36 | 2 | 0 | 163 |
| Douglas | 198 | -- | -- | -- | -- | 2 | -- | 181 |
| Franklin | 69 | -- | -- | -- | -- | 2 | -- | 61 |
| Gage | 13 | 0 | -- | -- | 0 | 0 | 2 | 5 |
| Greeley | 72 | 36 | -- | -- | 36 | -- | -- | 36 |
| Hall | 70 | 1 | -- | -- | 1 | 2 | -- | 61 |
| Hamilton | 1 | -- | -- | -- | -- | -- | 1 | -- |

Table 11.–Continued

| Forest Inventory Unit and county | All species | Cedar/ juniper | Ponderosa pine | White pine | Total softwoods | Ash | Black walnut | Cotton- wood |
|---|---|---|---|---|---|---|---|---|
| | | Softwoods | | | | Hardwoods | | |
| Howard | 72 | 36 | -- | -- | 36 | -- | -- | 36 |
| Jefferson | 4 | 1 | -- | -- | 1 | -- | 3 | -- |
| Johnson | 0 | -- | -- | -- | -- | -- | -- | -- |
| Kearney | 69 | -- | -- | -- | -- | 2 | -- | 61 |
| Lancaster | 99 | -- | -- | -- | -- | 1 | 1 | 91 |
| Madison | 92 | -- | -- | -- | -- | -- | -- | 92 |
| Merrick | 152 | 77 | -- | -- | 77 | 2 | -- | 73 |
| Nance | 110 | 37 | -- | -- | 37 | -- | -- | 72 |
| Nemaha | 10 | 0 | -- | -- | 0 | -- | 8 | 1 |
| Nuckolls | 0 | -- | -- | -- | -- | -- | -- | -- |
| Otoe | 7 | -- | -- | -- | -- | -- | 7 | -- |
| Pawnee | 3 | 0 | -- | -- | 0 | -- | 2 | -- |
| Phelps | 0 | 0 | -- | -- | 0 | -- | -- | -- |
| Pierce | 74 | -- | -- | -- | -- | -- | -- | 74 |
| Platte | 127 | 36 | -- | -- | 36 | -- | -- | 90 |
| Polk | 127 | 39 | -- | -- | 39 | 0 | 0 | 87 |
| Richardson | 35 | -- | -- | -- | -- | 0 | 25 | 5 |
| Saline | 13 | -- | -- | -- | -- | 0 | 2 | 5 |
| Sarpy | 197 | -- | -- | -- | -- | 2 | -- | 181 |
| Saunders | 771 | 0 | -- | -- | 0 | 3 | 0 | 755 |
| Seward | 7 | 1 | -- | -- | 1 | 1 | 3 | 0 |
| Sherman | 6 | 4 | 1 | -- | 6 | -- | -- | -- |
| Stanton | 33 | -- | -- | -- | -- | -- | -- | 33 |
| Thurston | 6 | -- | -- | -- | -- | -- | 6 | -- |

Table 11.—Continued

| Forest Inventory Unit and county | All species | Softwoods | | | | Hardwoods | | |
|---|---|---|---|---|---|---|---|---|
| | | Cedar/ juniper | Ponderosa pine | White pine | Total softwoods | Ash | Black walnut | Cotton- wood |
| Washington | 4 | -- | -- | -- | -- | -- | 4 | -- |
| Wayne | 129 | 0 | -- | -- | 0 | -- | -- | 129 |
| Webster | 70 | 0 | -- | -- | 0 | 2 | 0 | 61 |
| York | 14 | 5 | -- | 0 | 5 | 1 | 1 | 7 |
| Total | 3,956 | 352 | 2 | 0 | 354 | 29 | 68 | 3,393 |
| **Western Unit** | | | | | | | | |
| Antelope | 63 | 1 | 0 | -- | 1 | 0 | 0 | 62 |
| Brown | 16 | 16 | -- | -- | 16 | -- | -- | -- |
| Cherry | 19 | 7 | 11 | -- | 18 | 0 | 0 | -- |
| Cheyenne | 1 | -- | -- | -- | -- | -- | -- | 0 |
| Dawes | 179 | 1 | 178 | -- | 179 | -- | -- | -- |
| Holt | 1 | 1 | -- | -- | 1 | -- | -- | -- |
| Keya Paha | 100 | 19 | 81 | -- | 100 | 0 | 0 | -- |
| Kimball | 2 | -- | -- | -- | -- | 1 | -- | 1 |
| Knox | 27 | 7 | -- | -- | 7 | -- | 0 | 19 |
| Lincoln | 10 | 8 | 0 | -- | 8 | 1 | 0 | -- |
| Loup | 1 | 1 | -- | -- | 1 | -- | -- | -- |
| Rock | 5 | 5 | -- | -- | 5 | -- | -- | -- |
| Sheridan | 1 | -- | 1 | -- | -- | -- | -- | -- |
| Sioux | 173 | 0 | 172 | -- | 172 | -- | 1 | -- |
| Total | 597 | 66 | 443 | -- | 509 | 2 | 2 | 82 |
| State total | 4,553 | 417 | 445 | 0 | 863 | 30 | 70 | 3,475 |

Table 11.—Continued

| Forest Inventory Unit and county | | Hardwoods | | | | | | |
|---|---|---|---|---|---|---|---|---|
| | Elm | Hackberry | Soft maple | Red oak group | White oak group | Sycamore | Other hardwoods | Total hardwoods |
| **Eastern Unit** | | | | | | | | |
| Adams | 1 | -- | -- | -- | 4 | -- | -- | 69 |
| Boone | -- | -- | -- | -- | -- | -- | -- | 25 |
| Buffalo | 1 | -- | -- | -- | 5 | -- | -- | 72 |
| Burt | -- | -- | -- | -- | -- | -- | -- | 7 |
| Butler | -- | -- | -- | -- | 0 | -- | -- | 7 |
| Cass | -- | -- | -- | -- | -- | -- | -- | 0 |
| Cedar | -- | -- | -- | -- | -- | -- | -- | 147 |
| Clay | -- | -- | -- | -- | 0 | -- | -- | 0 |
| Colfax | -- | -- | -- | -- | -- | -- | -- | 153 |
| Cuming | -- | 0 | -- | -- | -- | -- | 0 | 18 |
| Custer | -- | -- | -- | -- | -- | -- | -- | 0 |
| Dakota | -- | -- | -- | -- | 0 | -- | -- | 371 |
| Dawson | -- | -- | -- | -- | -- | -- | -- | -- |
| Dixon | -- | -- | -- | -- | -- | -- | -- | 186 |
| Dodge | 1 | 0 | 1 | 0 | 5 | -- | 0 | 172 |
| Douglas | 2 | 1 | 2 | 1 | 9 | -- | 1 | 198 |
| Franklin | 1 | -- | -- | -- | 4 | -- | -- | 69 |
| Gage | 0 | 0 | 1 | -- | 3 | -- | -- | 12 |
| Greeley | -- | -- | -- | -- | -- | -- | -- | 36 |
| Hall | 1 | -- | -- | -- | 4 | -- | -- | 69 |
| Hamilton | -- | -- | -- | -- | -- | -- | -- | 1 |
| Howard | -- | -- | -- | -- | -- | -- | -- | 36 |
| Jefferson | -- | -- | -- | -- | 0 | -- | -- | 4 |

Table 11.—Continued

| Forest Inventory Unit and county | Elm | Hackberry | Soft maple | Hardwoods Red oak group | White oak group | Sycamore | Other hardwoods | Total hardwoods |
|---|---|---|---|---|---|---|---|---|
| Johnson | -- | -- | -- | -- | -- | -- | 0 | 0 |
| Kearney | 1 | -- | -- | -- | 4 | -- | 0 | 69 |
| Lancaster | 1 | 0 | 1 | -- | 4 | -- | 0 | 99 |
| Madison | -- | -- | -- | -- | -- | -- | -- | 92 |
| Merrick | -- | -- | -- | -- | -- | -- | -- | 75 |
| Nance | -- | -- | -- | -- | 0 | -- | -- | 72 |
| Nemaha | -- | -- | -- | 0 | -- | -- | 0 | 9 |
| Nuckolls | -- | -- | -- | -- | 0 | -- | -- | 0 |
| Otoe | -- | -- | -- | -- | -- | -- | -- | 7 |
| Pawnee | -- | -- | -- | -- | 1 | -- | 0 | 3 |
| Phelps | -- | -- | -- | -- | -- | -- | -- | -- |
| Pierce | -- | -- | -- | -- | -- | -- | -- | 74 |
| Platte | -- | -- | -- | -- | -- | -- | -- | 90 |
| Polk | 0 | -- | -- | -- | -- | -- | -- | 88 |
| Richardson | -- | -- | 1 | 1 | 3 | 0 | -- | 35 |
| Saline | 0 | -- | 2 | -- | 3 | -- | -- | 13 |
| Sarpy | 2 | 1 | 2 | -- | 9 | -- | 1 | 197 |
| Saunders | 2 | 1 | 2 | -- | 9 | -- | 1 | 771 |
| Seward | 0 | 0 | 0 | -- | 1 | -- | -- | 6 |
| Sherman | -- | -- | -- | -- | -- | -- | -- | -- |
| Stanton | -- | -- | -- | -- | -- | -- | -- | 33 |
| Thurston | -- | -- | -- | -- | -- | -- | -- | 6 |

Table 11.—Continued

|  | Hardwoods | | | | | | | |
| Forest Inventory Unit and county | Elm | Hackberry | Soft maple | Red oak group | White oak group | Sycamore | Other hardwoods | Total hardwoods |
|---|---|---|---|---|---|---|---|---|
| Washington | -- | -- | -- | -- | 0 | -- | -- | 4 |
| Wayne | -- | -- | -- | -- | 0 | -- | -- | 129 |
| Webster | 2 | 0 | 0 | -- | 4 | -- | 0 | 69 |
| York | -- | -- | -- | -- | 1 | -- | -- | 9 |
| Total | 15 | 5 | 11 | 2 | 75 | 0 | 4 | 3,602 |
| **Western Unit** | | | | | | | | |
| Antelope | -- | -- | -- | -- | 0 | -- | -- | 62 |
| Brown | -- | -- | -- | -- | -- | -- | 0 | 0 |
| Cherry | -- | -- | -- | -- | 0 | -- | -- | 1 |
| Cheyenne | 0 | -- | -- | -- | -- | -- | -- | 1 |
| Dawes | -- | -- | -- | -- | -- | -- | -- | -- |
| Holt | -- | -- | -- | -- | -- | -- | -- | -- |
| Keya Paha | -- | -- | -- | -- | 0 | -- | -- | 1 |
| Kimball | 0 | -- | -- | -- | -- | -- | -- | 2 |
| Knox | -- | -- | -- | -- | -- | -- | -- | 20 |
| Lincoln | -- | 0 | -- | -- | -- | -- | -- | 1 |
| Loup | -- | -- | -- | -- | -- | -- | -- | -- |
| Rock | -- | -- | -- | -- | -- | -- | -- | -- |
| Sheridan | -- | -- | -- | -- | -- | -- | -- | -- |
| Sioux | -- | -- | -- | -- | -- | -- | -- | 1 |
| Total | 1 | 0 | -- | -- | 1 | -- | 0 | 88 |
| State total | 16 | 5 | 11 | 2 | 75 | 0 | 5 | 3,690 |

*All table cells without observations are indicated by -- . Table value of 0 indicates the volume rounds to less than 1 thousand cubic feet. Columns and rows may not add to their totals due to rounding.*

Table 12.–Sawtimber removals from timberland for industrial roundwood, in thousand board feet, International ¼-inch rule, by Forest Inventory Unit, county, and species group, Nebraska, 2009

| Forest Inventory Unit and county | All species | Softwoods | | | | Hardwoods | | |
| | | Cedar/ juniper | Ponderosa pine | White pine | Total softwoods | Ash | Black walnut | Cotton- wood |
|---|---|---|---|---|---|---|---|---|
| **Eastern Unit** | | | | | | | | |
| Adams | 395 | -- | -- | -- | -- | 10 | -- | 361 |
| Boone | 150 | 2 | -- | -- | 2 | -- | -- | 147 |
| Buffalo | 411 | 1 | -- | -- | 1 | 10 | 1 | 372 |
| Burt | 40 | -- | -- | -- | -- | -- | -- | 40 |
| Butler | 36 | 1 | -- | -- | 1 | -- | 2 | 31 |
| Cass | 2 | -- | -- | -- | -- | -- | 2 | -- |
| Cedar | 869 | 2 | -- | -- | 2 | -- | -- | 867 |
| Clay | 0 | -- | -- | -- | -- | -- | -- | -- |
| Colfax | 976 | 192 | -- | -- | 192 | -- | -- | 784 |
| Cuming | 115 | 4 | 3 | -- | 7 | 3 | -- | 101 |
| Custer | 1 | 1 | -- | -- | 1 | -- | 1 | -- |
| Dakota | 2,186 | -- | -- | -- | -- | -- | 2 | 2,182 |
| Dawson | 0 | 0 | -- | -- | 0 | -- | -- | -- |
| Dixon | 1,098 | 1 | -- | -- | 1 | -- | 1 | 1,096 |
| Dodge | 1,153 | 192 | -- | 0 | 192 | 7 | 2 | 918 |
| Douglas | 1,146 | -- | -- | -- | -- | 12 | -- | 1,070 |
| Franklin | 397 | -- | -- | -- | -- | 10 | -- | 361 |
| Gage | 68 | 1 | -- | -- | 1 | 2 | 15 | 29 |
| Greeley | 383 | 192 | -- | -- | 192 | -- | -- | 192 |
| Hall | 401 | 4 | -- | -- | 4 | 10 | -- | 361 |
| Hamilton | 4 | -- | -- | -- | -- | -- | 4 | -- |

Table 12.—Continued

| Forest Inventory Unit and county | All species | Softwoods | | | | Hardwoods | | |
|---|---|---|---|---|---|---|---|---|
| | | Cedar/ juniper | Ponderosa pine | White pine | Total softwoods | Ash | Black walnut | Cotton- wood |
| Howard | 383 | 192 | -- | -- | 192 | -- | -- | 192 |
| Jefferson | 26 | 3 | -- | -- | 3 | -- | 22 | -- |
| Johnson | 1 | -- | -- | -- | -- | -- | -- | -- |
| Kearney | 394 | -- | -- | -- | -- | 10 | -- | 361 |
| Lancaster | 576 | -- | -- | -- | -- | 6 | 4 | 535 |
| Madison | 542 | -- | -- | -- | -- | -- | -- | 542 |
| Merrick | 803 | 404 | -- | -- | 404 | 12 | -- | 387 |
| Nance | 577 | 192 | -- | -- | 192 | -- | -- | 383 |
| Nemaha | 59 | 1 | -- | -- | 1 | -- | 53 | 3 |
| Nuckolls | 0 | -- | -- | -- | -- | -- | -- | -- |
| Otoe | 41 | -- | -- | -- | -- | -- | 41 | -- |
| Pawnee | 18 | 1 | -- | -- | 1 | -- | 12 | -- |
| Phelps | 1 | 1 | -- | -- | 1 | -- | -- | -- |
| Pierce | 434 | -- | -- | -- | -- | -- | -- | 434 |
| Platte | 685 | 192 | -- | -- | 192 | -- | -- | 493 |
| Polk | 670 | 207 | -- | -- | 207 | 1 | 2 | 458 |
| Richardson | 207 | -- | -- | -- | -- | 1 | 157 | 27 |
| Saline | 68 | -- | -- | -- | -- | 1 | 12 | 29 |
| Sarpy | 1,144 | -- | -- | -- | -- | 12 | -- | 1,070 |
| Saunders | 3,995 | 1 | -- | -- | 1 | 12 | 1 | 3,918 |
| Seward | 40 | 7 | -- | -- | 7 | 4 | 19 | 1 |
| Sherman | 27 | 20 | 7 | -- | 27 | -- | -- | -- |
| Stanton | 195 | -- | -- | -- | -- | -- | -- | 195 |

Table 12.–Continued

| Forest Inventory Unit and county | Softwoods | | | | | Hardwoods | | |
| --- | --- | --- | --- | --- | --- | --- | --- | --- |
| | All species | Cedar/ juniper | Ponderosa pine | White pine | Total softwoods | Ash | Black walnut | Cotton- wood |
| Thurston | 38 | -- | -- | -- | -- | -- | 38 | -- |
| Washington | 28 | -- | -- | -- | -- | -- | 28 | -- |
| Wayne | 761 | 1 | -- | -- | 1 | -- | -- | 759 |
| Webster | 400 | 2 | -- | -- | 2 | 10 | 0 | 361 |
| York | 74 | 23 | -- | -- | 23 | 4 | 6 | 39 |
| Total | 22,019 | 1,840 | 10 | 0 | 1,850 | 138 | 425 | 19,102 |
| **Western Unit** | | | | | | | | |
| Antelope | 369 | 3 | 1 | -- | 4 | 0 | 1 | 363 |
| Brown | 73 | 71 | -- | -- | 71 | -- | -- | -- |
| Cherry | 95 | 30 | 59 | -- | 90 | 1 | 2 | -- |
| Cheyenne | 4 | -- | -- | -- | -- | -- | -- | 3 |
| Dawes | 955 | 4 | 950 | -- | 955 | -- | -- | -- |
| Holt | 1 | 1 | -- | -- | 1 | -- | -- | -- |
| Keya Paha | 520 | 84 | 433 | -- | 516 | 1 | 2 | -- |
| Kimball | 10 | -- | -- | -- | -- | 3 | -- | 4 |
| Knox | 147 | 31 | -- | -- | 31 | -- | 1 | 114 |
| Lincoln | 43 | 35 | 1 | -- | 36 | 3 | 2 | -- |
| Loup | 7 | 7 | -- | -- | 7 | -- | -- | -- |
| Rock | 20 | 20 | -- | -- | 20 | -- | -- | -- |
| Sheridan | 4 | -- | 4 | -- | 4 | -- | -- | -- |
| Sioux | 924 | 2 | 917 | -- | 919 | -- | 6 | -- |
| Total | 3,170 | 288 | 2,367 | -- | 2,654 | 9 | 14 | 484 |
| State total | 25,189 | 2,128 | 2,377 | 0 | 4,504 | 147 | 439 | 19,587 |

Table 12.–Continued

| Forest Inventory Unit and county | Hardwoods | | | | | | | | Total hardwoods |
|---|---|---|---|---|---|---|---|---|---|
| | Elm | Hackberry | Soft maple | Red oak group | White oak group | Sycamore | Other hardwoods | | |

**Eastern Unit**

| | | | | | | | | | |
|---|---|---|---|---|---|---|---|---|---|
| Adams | 6 | -- | -- | -- | 17 | -- | -- | | 395 |
| Boone | -- | -- | -- | -- | -- | -- | -- | | 147 |
| Buffalo | 9 | -- | -- | -- | 18 | -- | -- | | 410 |
| Burt | -- | -- | -- | -- | -- | -- | -- | | 40 |
| Butler | -- | -- | -- | -- | 1 | -- | -- | | 34 |
| Cass | -- | -- | -- | -- | -- | -- | -- | | 2 |
| Cedar | -- | -- | -- | -- | -- | -- | -- | | 867 |
| Clay | -- | -- | -- | -- | 0 | -- | -- | | 0 |
| Colfax | -- | -- | -- | -- | -- | -- | -- | | 784 |
| Cuming | -- | 2 | -- | -- | -- | -- | 1 | | 108 |
| Custer | -- | -- | -- | -- | -- | -- | -- | | 1 |
| Dakota | -- | -- | -- | -- | 2 | -- | -- | | 2,186 |
| Dawson | -- | -- | -- | -- | -- | -- | -- | | -- |
| Dixon | -- | -- | -- | -- | -- | -- | -- | | 1,097 |
| Dodge | 5 | 2 | 5 | 1 | 18 | -- | 2 | | 961 |
| Douglas | 10 | 5 | 10 | 2 | 33 | -- | 5 | | 1,146 |
| Franklin | 9 | -- | -- | -- | 16 | -- | -- | | 397 |
| Gage | 1 | 2 | 7 | -- | 11 | -- | -- | | 67 |
| Greeley | -- | -- | -- | -- | -- | -- | -- | | 192 |
| Hall | 9 | -- | -- | -- | 16 | -- | -- | | 397 |
| Hamilton | -- | -- | -- | -- | -- | -- | -- | | 4 |
| Howard | -- | -- | -- | -- | -- | -- | -- | | 192 |

Table 12.—Continued

| Forest Inventory Unit and county | Hardwoods | | | | | | | Total hardwoods |
| --- | --- | --- | --- | --- | --- | --- | --- | --- |
| | Elm | Hackberry | Soft maple | Red oak group | White oak group | Sycamore | Other hardwoods | |
| Jefferson | -- | -- | -- | -- | 1 | -- | -- | 23 |
| Johnson | -- | -- | -- | -- | -- | -- | 1 | 1 |
| Kearney | 6 | -- | -- | -- | 16 | -- | -- | 394 |
| Lancaster | 5 | 2 | 5 | -- | 16 | -- | 2 | 576 |
| Madison | -- | -- | -- | -- | -- | -- | -- | 542 |
| Merrick | -- | -- | -- | -- | -- | -- | -- | 399 |
| Nance | -- | -- | -- | -- | 2 | -- | -- | 385 |
| Nemaha | -- | -- | -- | 1 | -- | -- | 1 | 58 |
| Nuckolls | -- | -- | -- | -- | 0 | -- | -- | 0 |
| Otoe | -- | -- | -- | -- | -- | -- | -- | 41 |
| Pawnee | -- | -- | -- | -- | 4 | -- | 1 | 17 |
| Phelps | -- | -- | -- | -- | -- | -- | -- | -- |
| Pierce | -- | -- | -- | -- | -- | -- | -- | 434 |
| Platte | -- | -- | -- | -- | -- | -- | -- | 493 |
| Polk | 1 | -- | -- | -- | -- | -- | -- | 463 |
| Richardson | -- | -- | 4 | 5 | 10 | 3 | -- | 207 |
| Saline | 1 | -- | 12 | -- | 12 | -- | -- | 68 |
| Sarpy | 10 | 5 | 10 | -- | 33 | -- | 5 | 1,144 |
| Saunders | 10 | 5 | 10 | -- | 34 | -- | 5 | 3,994 |
| Seward | 1 | 2 | 2 | -- | 3 | -- | -- | 33 |
| Sherman | -- | -- | -- | -- | -- | -- | -- | -- |
| Stanton | -- | -- | -- | -- | -- | -- | -- | 195 |
| Thurston | -- | -- | -- | -- | -- | -- | -- | 38 |

Table 12.–Continued

| Forest Inventory Unit and county | Elm | Hackberry | Soft maple | Red oak group | White oak group | Sycamore | Other hardwoods | Total hardwoods |
|---|---|---|---|---|---|---|---|---|
| Washington | -- | -- | -- | -- | 0 | -- | -- | 28 |
| Wayne | -- | -- | -- | -- | 1 | -- | -- | 760 |
| Webster | 9 | 0 | 0 | -- | 17 | -- | 0 | 398 |
| York | -- | -- | -- | -- | 3 | -- | -- | 52 |
| Total | 90 | 27 | 65 | 9 | 285 | 3 | 24 | 20,168 |
| **Western Unit** | | | | | | | | |
| Antelope | -- | -- | -- | -- | 1 | -- | -- | 365 |
| Brown | -- | -- | -- | -- | -- | -- | 1 | 1 |
| Cherry | -- | -- | -- | -- | 1 | -- | -- | 5 |
| Cheyenne | 1 | -- | -- | -- | -- | -- | -- | 4 |
| Dawes | -- | -- | -- | -- | -- | -- | -- | -- |
| Holt | -- | -- | -- | -- | -- | -- | -- | -- |
| Keya Paha | -- | -- | -- | -- | 0 | -- | -- | 4 |
| Kimball | 2 | -- | -- | -- | -- | -- | -- | 10 |
| Knox | -- | -- | -- | -- | -- | -- | -- | 115 |
| Lincoln | -- | 2 | -- | -- | -- | -- | -- | 7 |
| Loup | -- | -- | -- | -- | -- | -- | -- | -- |
| Rock | -- | -- | -- | -- | -- | -- | -- | -- |
| Sheridan | -- | -- | -- | -- | -- | -- | -- | -- |
| Sioux | -- | -- | -- | -- | -- | -- | -- | 6 |
| Total | 4 | 2 | -- | -- | 2 | -- | 1 | 516 |
| State total | 93 | 29 | 65 | 9 | 287 | 3 | 25 | 20,685 |

*All table cells without observations are indicated by — . Table value of 0 indicates the volume rounds to less than 1 thousand board feet. Columns and rows may not add to their totals due to rounding.*

Table 13.—Harvest residue generated by industrial roundwood harvesting, in thousand cubic feet, by Forest Inventory Unit, county, and species group, Nebraska, 2009

| Forest Inventory Unit and county | All species | Softwoods | | | | Hardwoods | | |
|---|---|---|---|---|---|---|---|---|
| | | Cedar/ juniper | Ponderosa pine | White pine | Total softwoods | Ash | Black walnut | Cotton- wood |
| **Eastern Unit** | | | | | | | | |
| Adams | 31 | -- | -- | -- | -- | 1 | -- | 27 |
| Boone | 11 | 0 | -- | -- | 0 | -- | -- | 11 |
| Buffalo | 32 | 0 | -- | -- | 0 | 1 | 0 | 27 |
| Burt | 3 | -- | -- | -- | -- | -- | -- | 3 |
| Butler | 2 | 0 | -- | -- | 0 | -- | 0 | 2 |
| Cass | 0 | -- | -- | -- | -- | -- | 0 | -- |
| Cedar | 64 | 0 | -- | -- | 0 | -- | -- | 64 |
| Clay | 0 | -- | -- | -- | -- | -- | -- | -- |
| Colfax | 37 | 4 | -- | -- | 4 | -- | -- | 33 |
| Cuming | 8 | 0 | 0 | -- | 0 | 0 | -- | 7 |
| Custer | 0 | 0 | -- | -- | 0 | -- | 0 | -- |
| Dakota | 161 | -- | -- | -- | -- | -- | 0 | 161 |
| Dawson | 0 | 0 | -- | -- | 0 | -- | -- | -- |
| Dixon | 81 | 0 | -- | -- | 0 | -- | 0 | 81 |
| Dodge | 55 | 4 | -- | 0 | 4 | 1 | 0 | 47 |
| Douglas | 87 | -- | -- | -- | -- | 1 | 1 | 79 |
| Franklin | 31 | -- | -- | -- | -- | 1 | -- | 27 |
| Gage | 6 | 0 | -- | -- | 0 | 0 | 1 | 2 |
| Greeley | 8 | 4 | -- | -- | 4 | 0 | -- | 4 |
| Hall | 31 | 0 | -- | -- | 0 | 1 | -- | 27 |
| Hamilton | 0 | -- | -- | -- | -- | -- | 0 | -- |
| Howard | 8 | 4 | -- | -- | 4 | -- | -- | 4 |

Table 13.–Continued

| Forest Inventory Unit and county | All species | Softwoods | | | | Hardwoods | | |
|---|---|---|---|---|---|---|---|---|
| | | Cedar/ juniper | Ponderosa pine | White pine | Total softwoods | Ash | Black walnut | Cotton- wood |
| Jefferson | 2 | 0 | -- | -- | 0 | -- | 1 | -- |
| Johnson | 0 | -- | -- | -- | -- | -- | -- | -- |
| Kearney | 30 | -- | -- | -- | -- | 1 | -- | 27 |
| Lancaster | 44 | -- | -- | -- | -- | 1 | 0 | 39 |
| Madison | 40 | -- | -- | -- | -- | -- | -- | 40 |
| Merrick | 18 | 9 | -- | -- | 9 | 1 | -- | 8 |
| Nance | 12 | 4 | -- | -- | 4 | -- | -- | 8 |
| Nemaha | 3 | 0 | -- | -- | 0 | -- | 3 | 0 |
| Nuckolls | 0 | -- | -- | -- | -- | -- | -- | -- |
| Otoe | 2 | -- | -- | -- | -- | -- | 2 | -- |
| Pawnee | 1 | 0 | -- | -- | 0 | -- | 1 | -- |
| Phelps | 0 | 0 | -- | -- | 0 | -- | -- | -- |
| Pierce | 32 | -- | -- | -- | -- | -- | -- | 32 |
| Platte | 19 | 4 | -- | -- | 4 | -- | -- | 16 |
| Polk | 18 | 5 | -- | -- | 5 | 0 | 0 | 12 |
| Richardson | 14 | -- | -- | -- | -- | 0 | 9 | 2 |
| Saline | 6 | -- | -- | -- | -- | 0 | 1 | 2 |
| Sarpy | 87 | -- | -- | -- | -- | 1 | -- | 79 |
| Saunders | 267 | 0 | -- | -- | 0 | 1 | 0 | 259 |
| Seward | 3 | 1 | -- | -- | 1 | 0 | 1 | 0 |
| Sherman | 2 | 2 | 0 | -- | 2 | -- | -- | -- |
| Stanton | 14 | -- | -- | -- | -- | -- | -- | 14 |

Table 13.–Continued

| Forest Inventory Unit and county | Softwoods | | | | | Hardwoods | | |
|---|---|---|---|---|---|---|---|---|
| | All species | Cedar/ juniper | Ponderosa pine | White pine | Total softwoods | Ash | Black walnut | Cotton- wood |
| Thurston | 2 | -- | -- | -- | -- | -- | 2 | -- |
| Washington | 2 | -- | -- | -- | -- | -- | 2 | -- |
| Wayne | 56 | 0 | -- | -- | 0 | -- | -- | 56 |
| Webster | 31 | 0 | -- | -- | 0 | 1 | 0 | 27 |
| York | 6 | 2 | -- | -- | 2 | 0 | 0 | 3 |
| Total | 1,366 | 43 | 0 | 0 | 44 | 16 | 24 | 1,227 |
| **Western Unit** | | | | | | | | |
| Antelope | 27 | 0 | 0 | -- | 0 | 0 | 0 | 27 |
| Brown | 6 | 6 | -- | -- | 6 | -- | -- | -- |
| Cherry | 5 | 2 | 3 | -- | 5 | 0 | 0 | -- |
| Cheyenne | 0 | 0 | -- | -- | -- | -- | -- | 0 |
| Dawes | 43 | 0 | 42 | -- | 43 | -- | -- | -- |
| Holt | 0 | 0 | -- | -- | 0 | -- | -- | -- |
| Keya Paha | 17 | 7 | 10 | -- | 16 | 0 | 0 | -- |
| Kimball | 1 | 0 | -- | -- | -- | 0 | -- | 0 |
| Knox | 11 | 3 | -- | -- | 3 | -- | 0 | 8 |
| Lincoln | 3 | 3 | 0 | -- | 3 | 0 | 0 | -- |
| Loup | 1 | 1 | -- | -- | 1 | -- | -- | -- |
| Rock | 2 | 2 | -- | -- | 2 | -- | -- | -- |
| Sheridan | 0 | 0 | 0 | -- | 0 | -- | -- | -- |
| Sioux | 41 | 0 | 41 | -- | 41 | -- | -- | -- |
| Total | 157 | 23 | 96 | 0 | 119 | 17 | 1 | 36 |
| State total | 1,523 | 66 | 96 | 0 | 162 | 17 | 25 | 1,262 |

Table 13.–Continued

| Forest Inventory Unit and county | Elm | Hackberry | Soft maple | Red oak group | White oak group | Sycamore | Other hardwoods | Total hardwoods |
|---|---|---|---|---|---|---|---|---|
| **Eastern Unit** | | | | | | | | |
| Adams | 0 | -- | -- | -- | 2 | -- | -- | 31 |
| Boone | -- | -- | -- | -- | -- | -- | -- | 11 |
| Buffalo | 1 | -- | -- | -- | 3 | -- | -- | 32 |
| Burt | -- | -- | -- | -- | -- | -- | -- | 3 |
| Butler | -- | -- | -- | -- | 0 | -- | -- | 2 |
| Cass | -- | -- | -- | -- | -- | -- | -- | 0 |
| Cedar | -- | -- | -- | -- | -- | -- | -- | 64 |
| Clay | -- | -- | -- | -- | 0 | -- | -- | 0 |
| Colfax | -- | -- | -- | -- | -- | -- | -- | 33 |
| Cuming | -- | 0 | -- | -- | -- | -- | 0 | 8 |
| Custer | -- | -- | -- | -- | -- | -- | -- | 0 |
| Dakota | -- | -- | -- | -- | 0 | -- | -- | 161 |
| Dawson | -- | -- | -- | -- | -- | -- | -- | -- |
| Dixon | -- | -- | -- | -- | -- | -- | -- | 81 |
| Dodge | 0 | 0 | 0 | 0 | 3 | -- | 0 | 52 |
| Douglas | 1 | 0 | 1 | 0 | 5 | -- | 0 | 87 |
| Franklin | 1 | -- | -- | -- | 2 | -- | -- | 31 |
| Gage | 0 | 0 | 1 | -- | 1 | -- | -- | 5 |
| Greeley | -- | -- | -- | -- | -- | -- | -- | 4 |
| Hall | 1 | -- | -- | -- | 2 | -- | -- | 31 |
| Hamilton | -- | -- | -- | -- | -- | -- | -- | 0 |
| Howard | -- | -- | -- | -- | -- | -- | -- | 4 |

Table 13.–Continued

|  | Hardwoods | | | | | | | |
| Forest Inventory Unit and county | Elm | Hackberry | Soft maple | Red oak group | White oak group | Sycamore | Other hardwoods | Total hardwoods |
|---|---|---|---|---|---|---|---|---|
| Jefferson | -- | -- | -- | -- | 0 | -- | -- | 1 |
| Johnson | -- | -- | -- | -- | -- | -- | 0 | 0 |
| Kearney | 0 | -- | -- | -- | 2 | -- | -- | 30 |
| Lancaster | 0 | 0 | 0 | -- | 2 | -- | 0 | 44 |
| Madison | -- | -- | -- | -- | -- | -- | -- | 40 |
| Merrick | -- | -- | -- | -- | -- | -- | -- | 9 |
| Nance | -- | -- | -- | -- | 0 | -- | -- | 8 |
| Nemaha | -- | -- | -- | 0 | -- | -- | 0 | 3 |
| Nuckolls | -- | -- | -- | -- | 0 | -- | -- | 0 |
| Otoe | -- | -- | -- | -- | -- | -- | -- | 2 |
| Pawnee | -- | -- | -- | -- | 1 | -- | 0 | 1 |
| Phelps | -- | -- | -- | -- | -- | -- | -- | -- |
| Pierce | -- | -- | -- | -- | -- | -- | -- | 32 |
| Platte | -- | -- | -- | -- | -- | -- | -- | 16 |
| Polk | 0 | -- | -- | -- | -- | -- | -- | 13 |
| Richardson | -- | -- | 0 | 1 | 1 | 0 | -- | 14 |
| Saline | 0 | -- | 1 | -- | 2 | -- | -- | 6 |
| Sarpy | 1 | 0 | 1 | -- | 5 | -- | 0 | 87 |
| Saunders | 1 | 0 | 1 | -- | 5 | -- | 0 | 267 |
| Seward | 0 | 0 | 0 | -- | 0 | -- | -- | 2 |
| Sherman | -- | -- | -- | -- | -- | -- | -- | -- |
| Stanton | -- | -- | -- | -- | -- | -- | -- | 14 |
| Thurston | -- | -- | -- | -- | -- | -- | -- | 2 |

Table 13.—Continued

|  | Hardwoods | | | | | | | |
| Forest Inventory Unit and county | Elm | Hackberry | Soft maple | Red oak group | White oak group | Sycamore | Other hardwoods | Total hardwoods |
|---|---|---|---|---|---|---|---|---|
| Washington | -- | -- | -- | -- | 0 | -- | -- | 2 |
| Wayne | -- | -- | -- | -- | 0 | -- | -- | 56 |
| Webster | 1 | 0 | 0 | -- | 2 | -- | 0 | 31 |
| York | -- | -- | -- | -- | 0 | -- | -- | 4 |
| Total | 6 | 2 | 5 | 1 | 39 | 0 | 2 | 1,322 |
| **Western Unit** | | | | | | | | |
| Antelope | -- | -- | -- | -- | 0 | -- | -- | 27 |
| Brown | -- | -- | -- | -- | 0 | -- | 0 | 0 |
| Cherry | -- | -- | -- | -- | 0 | -- | -- | 0 |
| Cheyenne | 0 | -- | -- | -- | -- | -- | -- | 0 |
| Dawes | -- | -- | -- | -- | -- | -- | -- | -- |
| Holt | -- | -- | -- | -- | -- | -- | -- | -- |
| Keya Paha | -- | -- | -- | -- | 0 | -- | -- | 0 |
| Kimball | 0 | -- | -- | -- | -- | -- | -- | 1 |
| Knox | -- | -- | -- | -- | -- | -- | -- | 8 |
| Lincoln | -- | 0 | -- | -- | -- | -- | -- | 1 |
| Loup | -- | -- | -- | -- | -- | -- | -- | -- |
| Rock | -- | -- | -- | -- | -- | -- | -- | -- |
| Sheridan | -- | -- | -- | -- | -- | -- | -- | -- |
| Sioux | -- | -- | -- | -- | -- | -- | -- | 0 |
| Total | 0 | 0 | -- | -- | 0 | -- | 0 | 38 |
| State total | 7 | 2 | 5 | 1 | 40 | 0 | 2 | 1,361 |

All table cells without observations are indicated by --. Table value of 0 indicates the volume rounds to less than 1 thousand cubic feet. Columns and rows may not add to their totals due to rounding.

Table 14.–Disposition of residues produced at primary wood-using mills, in green tons, by Forest Inventory Unit, disposition, residue type, and softwoods and hardwoods, Nebraska, 2009

| Forest Inventory Unit and disposition | Total all residues | | Residue type | | | | | | | |
|---|---|---|---|---|---|---|---|---|---|---|
| | | | Total wood residue | | Wood residue | | | | Bark | |
| | | | | | Coarse[a] | | Fine[b] | | | |
| | Softwood | Hardwood | Softwood | Hardwood | Softwood | Hardwood | Softwood | Hardwood | Softwood | Hardwood |
| **All Units** | | | | | | | | | | |
| Industrial fuel | 1,918 | 10,020 | 1,912 | 10,014 | 203 | 5,640 | 1,708 | 4,374 | 7 | 6 |
| Residential fuel | 289 | 290 | 232 | 204 | 229 | 204 | 3 | 3 | 57 | 85 |
| Mulch | 24 | 26,448 | 15 | 18,616 | 4 | 13,051 | 11 | 5,565 | 9 | 7,833 |
| Miscellaneous[c] | 217 | 13,079 | 213 | 10,876 | 131 | 5,800 | 83 | 5,076 | 3 | 2,203 |
| Not used | 4,437 | 11,669 | 3,423 | 8,655 | 3,192 | 6,803 | 230 | 1,851 | 1,014 | 3,015 |
| Total | 6,884 | 61,506 | 5,795 | 48,365 | 3,760 | 31,498 | 2,035 | 16,867 | 1,089 | 13,141 |
| **Eastern Unit** | | | | | | | | | | |
| Industrial fuel | 1,894 | 10,020 | 1,888 | 10,014 | 179 | 5,640 | 1,708 | 4,374 | 7 | 6 |
| Residential fuel | 98 | 275 | 76 | 194 | 76 | 194 | -- | -- | 22 | 81 |
| Mulch | 24 | 26,448 | 15 | 18,616 | 4 | 13,051 | 11 | 5,565 | 9 | 7,833 |
| Miscellaneous[c] | 42 | 13,077 | 38 | 10,874 | 11 | 5,800 | 28 | 5,074 | 3 | 2,203 |
| Not used | 3,984 | 11,494 | 3,093 | 8,520 | 2,980 | 6,708 | 113 | 1,812 | 891 | 2,973 |
| Total | 6,041 | 61,315 | 5,110 | 48,218 | 3,250 | 31,393 | 1,860 | 16,825 | 931 | 13,096 |
| **Western Unit** | | | | | | | | | | |
| Industrial fuel | 24 | -- | 24 | -- | 24 | -- | -- | -- | -- | -- |
| Residential fuel | 191 | 14 | 156 | 10 | 153 | 10 | 3 | -- | 35 | 4 |
| Miscellaneous[c] | 175 | 2 | 175 | 2 | 120 | -- | 55 | 2 | -- | -- |
| Not used | 452 | 175 | 330 | 134 | 213 | 95 | 117 | 39 | 123 | 41 |
| Total | 843 | 192 | 685 | 147 | 510 | 105 | 175 | 42 | 158 | 45 |

[a] Suitable for chipping such as slabs, edgings, veneer cores, etc.
[b] Not suitable for chipping such as sawdust, veneer clippings etc.
[c] Livestock bedding, small dimension, specialty items, etc.
*Table may not sum due to rounding.*